THE BRITISH ISLES

Foreword by
His Grace, The Duke of Norfolk, C.B., C.B.E., M.C.
Earl Marshal of England

VIKING

VIKING

Penguin Books Canada Ltd., 2801 John Street, Markham, Ontario, Canada L3R 1B4
Penguin Books, Harmondsworth, Middlesex, England
Viking Penguin Inc., 40 West 23rd Street, New York, New York 10010 U.S.A.
Penguin Books Australia Ltd., Ringwood, Victoria, Australia
Penguin Books (N.Z.) Ltd., 182-190 Wairau Road, Auckland 10, New Zealand

First published in Canada by Penguin Books Canada Limited, 1988

Printed and bound in Barcelona, Spain by Cronion, S.A..

Canadian Cataloguing in Publication Data

Msiad, Philip Clucas
    The British Isles

ISBN 0-670-81920-4

1.   Great Britain – Description and travel –
1971–   Views.   I. Title

DA667.M78 1987   941'.002'22   C87–093655–7

Foreword

Tourists visiting Britain are offered an historical feast, greater and more varied than any other European country can afford. This is because we have not been invaded since 1066, nor have we had the misfortune – at least since the days of Cromwell in 1649, or the flight of James II in 1688 – of resolving our government by resorting to revolution. Compare our good fortune with that of our neighbours France or Germany, ravaged by the Thirty Years' War, the Wars of the Spanish Succession, the Napoleonic Wars and the two World Wars this century. And reflect on the destruction of the buildings and treasures of France by the revolutions of 1789, 1848 and so on.

And one must add the subtler point that our insularity has preserved our primogeniture system of inheritance from the inevitable dispersal of family collections – and of many great castles and houses – which the Code Napoleon inflicted on continental families. Why, for instance, did President de Gaulle have to refurbish Versailles and the Grand Trianon with any 19th century pieces he could find, or have copies specially made? Because the furniture of the Bourbons resided in the Wallace Collection, Waddesden, Boughton and Drumlanrig. We, by contrast, have an incredible number of manor houses, carefully cherished by squires whose families have lived in them for generations and we can, as a result, boast living, local museums of incomparable historical importance.

Of course, much superstitious clutter was destroyed during the Reformation, and at the hands of the Puritans, but at least the glorious medieval cathedrals and village churches were left standing. Alas, the Dissolution of the Monasteries in 1536 destroyed fine abbeys and priories, and we are left to ponder their significance in medieval Britain by musing over the gaunt ruins, such as those of Fountains and Rievaulx.

We have, admittedly, suffered by lack of space for our 56 million population, but the tourist can still see how the Romans landed on the south and east coasts, and how, first using sea communications and later, having built their roads, such as Ermine Street and Watling Street, they pushed the native Celts westwards to Wales and Cornwall and northwards to the Lake District and Scotland.

And if, in the years to come, a Chinese tourist visits us and boasts of his great Chin and Han Dynasties (200BC), or even the Shang and Hsian Dynasties (2,000 to 1,100BC), I hope he will visit Avebury and Stonehenge and marvel at the results of the inhabitants of Bronze Age Britain transporting the Bluestone pillars from the Prescelly Mountains in South Wales in the 17th century BC!

This large, beautifully presented volume provides a generous taste of Britain's architectural heritage as well as a survey of her coastal and inland beauty, and the warmth and variety of her town and village life. As you enjoy its colourful contents, remember that much of what we see today owes its existence and appearance to the events and philosophies of many centuries of continuous social development.

Norfolk.

Miles, 17th Duke of Norfolk

No country in the world is richer than Britain in its patchwork of natural beauty. It is a mélange formed by the play of light and shade upon the landscape, by the tones which moss, lichen and fern impart upon mellow stonework, by the placing of spired church or ruined castle within the scene, and by the memories that have been stitched into the fabric of her landscape – into thyme-scented downland and primrose-haunted hedgerow; into silver threads of stream and darkling reed-mere.

The landscape of England, Scotland and Wales is one of rich and subtle contrast, where variety is the key to abiding fascination, and upon which each season paints its own freshness – be it the sight of wind-racked elms beyond a cornfield, poppy-studded amid the harvest gold, and shimmering in a summer's haze; the smell of wild hops hanging thickly from autumn bine; a grey winter's landscape, grizzled by sleet, its chill solitude broken only by the harsh call of the crows; or by the first flush of springtide, whose yearly appearance seems to exude the very essence of pastoral verse –

> When weeds, in wheels, shoot long and lovely and lush;
> Thrush's eggs look little low heavens, and thrush
> Through the echoing timber does so rinse and wring
> The ear, it strikes like lightnings to hear him sing;
> The glassy peartree leaves and blooms, they brush
> The descending blue; that blue is all in a rush
> With richness; the racing lambs too have fair their fling.

With variety goes surprise. Britain is a country of happy surprises, and there is no need to travel far to be pleasantly astonished. In the West, among rounded hills and soft yielding pasture, one suddenly arrives at the bleak tablelands of Dartmoor and Exmoor; and at Glastonbury there is an unexpected extent of fen whose flatness seems to suggest the landscape of Cambridgeshire. The long green walls of the South and North Downs – with their far-reaching views over the oast-houses, hop fields and orchards of Kent – are equally joyful surprises: the Weald is another of them. East Anglia has a kind of rough heath country of its own, that one never expects to find there, but is always delighted to see. After the easy rolling meadows of the Shires, the dramatic Peak District with its steep scarp never fails to astonish, for it seems to have no business there. Similarly, to the north, there are remnants of the Ice Age in the flowers and shrubs of Teesdale – alpine gentians and juniper – whilst a short distance away drifts of bluebells, wood anemonies and wild garlic carpet the primeval woodlands that crowd the vales.

Another characteristic of the British landscape is its exquisite moderation – born of a compromise between wildness and tameness. Here the hand of nature and the works of man harmonize: the hedges, the wooden fences, even the low stone walls that bind the northern fells, all have been gently subdued by nature until at last they might have been natural growths themselves, like the mosses that cover their wood and stone. Indeed, man has no need to be ashamed of the extent of his handiwork – where in Devon he built his thatched cottages of colour-wash cob, where in Herefordshire he used his timber and plaster to such striking 'magpie-like' effect, or where in the grim north he built his grey peel towers as defence against raiders from across the border. It is no accident either that the works of our earliest ancestors – such as the tall stones of Callernish, the 'Druids' Circle at Keswick, or any mighty prehistoric earthwork like Maiden Castle or Uffington Hill Fort – stand in surroundings of peerless loveliness. Thus are built (at a later age) the Abbey of Tintern on the Wye, Dryburgh in the arm of the Tweed, Rievaulx in the green cup of the Hambledon Hills, and Fountains Abbey nestled amongst trees and rocks. Of similar merit are Durham Cathedral set high on its rock promontory overhanging the Wear, Lincoln overlooking half a county, and Ely poised triumphantly above the Fens. Nor was this sense of beauty lost with the first flush of enthu-siasm – that material prosperity did not blunt the medieval mind can be seen at a glance around any Cotswold village, where houses have an irregularity and colouring that make them fit snugly into the landscape as though they were as much a piece of natural history as the trees that shade them. Such landscapes are a comfort to man, yet the countryside has not relinquished all of its ancient savagery and power – the vast moors, the mountains and the cruel seascapes still hold him in awe.

The enormous variety of countryside to be found in Britain is what makes a journey through its landscape so infinitely rewarding. In the succeeding chapters this progression is charted, and encompasses all the regions of these enchanted Isles – from the magnificently divergent landscape of the Western shores, through the chalk downlands of Southern England, to the lush pasture and ploughland of East Anglia and the Fens. It journeys to the Cotswolds and Malvern Hills, to the gentle terrain of the vales and the Welsh borderlands, and into the remote fastnesses of the mountains of Wales. From the Shire country of England's heartland the warmth of the South is supplanted by the rugged grandeur of Lakeland, and the cold fells and sheltered dales of the North. The final chapters cross the Cheviots and the Roman Wall to the marcherlands and Southern uplands of Scotland, which in turn melt into the full glorious fury of the Highlands, whose dramatic scenery of remote mountains, lochs and islands are the equal of any.

The West Country
Land of Contrast and Rich Diversity

It is pleasant to think of the West Country – with its long coastline abutting the surging swell of two seas and the crashing breakers of the open ocean – as though it were a country in itself. Indeed, there is a sense in which it was always so, for since man first roamed these Isles the Plain of Somerset, with its all but impenetrable landscape of marsh and lagoon, has formed a barrier between the lands of Devon and Cornwall and the rest of England. Early lines of communication consisted of tortuous trackways which always followed the highest contour to avoid the steep fall of streams and the area's tidal estuaries. The trails through Somerset and Dorset, where they were low lying or progressed through forest, were virtually impassable; in some parts of these counties this remained true right up to the advent of the railways. Thus was born the West Countryman's close affinity with the wild waters of his native coastline (sea-voyage was less fraught with hazard than overland travel) forging that proud kinship with the sea that in Elizabethan times controlled the destiny of the English Realm.

Cornwall, Devon and Somerset are traditionally set apart from the bulk of England, yet these Lands of the West possess the widest diversity of scenery to be found anywhere in Britain – even within their own individual county borders. Thus are the broad, sweeping moorlands of Dartmoor, with its tors and denuded high rocks, contrasted by the mild estuaries of East Devon so close at hand. Similarly, the grandeur of Bodmin Moor to the West in Cornwall and the harsh granite cliffs of the sea-coast are the direct antipathy of the gentle 'lost' worlds where birds flash in the leaf-canopied sunlight of lanes that rise but half a mile from shore or mere: here lies the West Country's true beauty – a beauty of informality, of secret places where sweet violets, primroses, wild garlic and flowers without number mingle with moss and damp-scented fern: where lichen-covered trees grow in woodlands haunted by stonechat, and apple trees long abandoned to nature stoop heavily under the weight of autumn fruit. Such joys are largely a matter of glimpse and chance – always of the hidden byway – and unknown to strange eyes.

The variety of the Western Landscape is due, as it is everywhere, to the geological variety of its composition. The old red sandstone of northern Exmoor, with its rolling expanse of heath and bracken given over to centuries of wind and rain; or Dartmoor, with its peat-coloured streams that criss-cross the moor, creating areas of swamp – intensely green, yet very dangerous – bear an entirely different vegetation from the upper greensand of the Somerset Heights. These sweep down in silhouette against the southern sky to enclose wooded orchards and pastures: here the upland ash and the rhododendron flourish in profusion, and willows shed their characteristic melancholy onto the scene. It is a land of fertile alluvial plain – dotted with black-faced sheep, and ponies (the lineal descendants of the Anglo-Saxon 'wild horse') –

through which silver rivers flow quietly onward to the broad surges of the bar and the everlasting thunder of the long Atlantic swell.

Somerset is perhaps the most varied county of all. Nothing could be more perfect in contrast than the shaven slopes and lustrine cliffs of the Mendips and the rugged contours of the Bredon Hills and Exmoor – with its rounded heather knolls, the deep blue of its waters and the green woods above, where in April and early May chaffinches, wrens and willow warblers sing in coppice woodland lush with campion and royal fern. From the south of the county the frowning heights of Blackdown look straight across Taunton Dene to the gently swelling Quantocks – filled with the soul of Coleridge and Wordsworth – and the little hills of Polden which lie below Glastonbury and the marshes of Brue.

These marshlands, now reclaimed and fertile, tell their own story of the days when Athelney and Glastonbury Tor were still islands, and when ships sailed right up the Parrett River. These lands of Alfred's exile – during Wessex' lowest fortune – have a singular dark beauty of their own, which, like the beauty of the Fens, is largely one of cloud and sky – yet the black soil and crimson osier withes give them a sinister colour – bringing back memories of Monmouth and his ill-starred confederates as though the blood of armies still stained the earth.

Of an age older than Alfred – older even than Arthur and his sword Excalibur (which is said to rest in Dozmary Pool) – is Glastonbury, which sheds the light of its legends over the surrounding marshlands. It should not be forgotten that this first Christian Church in Britain was never destroyed by the heathen invader, and that the traditions of Glastonbury stretch back to the childhood of Christ Himself; that William Blake, when he asked:

> 'And did those feet in ancient time,
> Walk upon England's mountains green?
> And was the Holy Lamb of God
> On England's pleasant pastures seen?
> And did the Countenance Divine
> Shine forth upon our clouded hills?'

was referring to the green Mendip Hills. Here also, according to lore, Joseph of Arimathea journeyed to the pastures of Somerset, burying the Chalice of the Last Supper – the Holy Grail – under a spring on Glastonbury Tor.

In the West Country masons had at hand everything they needed in the nature of building stone. They followed the lead of those who built so faithfully at the Abbey of Glastonbury; and all the traditional changes in architectural style – from Saxon and Norman to Perpendicular style – can be followed in the Parish churches of Devon, Cornwall and Somerset. The High Gothic predominates, and many of the tallest church towers are likened to 'cold jewels set in a blaze of aquamarine that is the summer sky'. Such are Episcopi with its deep Norman porch, whose sandstone has been burnt red by fire; the magnificently proportioned tower of Evercrech, and the proud churches of Chewton, Mendip and Wrington.

Chalk Country
The Downland Plain and the Chilterns

No matter where you wander in the Chalk Country of Southern England you will be on the downs, or on the edge of them. The Chiltern Hills range in a south-westerly direction from Bedfordshire, through Hertfordshire and Buckinghamshire to end in Oxfordshire. Immediately across the valley of the grey-ribboned Thames the Berkshire Downs connect the Chilterns on the east with the Marlborough Downs to the west – a land of vague mists and rooks cawing above the plough. From here they run southerly to Salisbury Plain – with only the smiling valley of the Pewsey Vale to break their rolling majestic range – from where they tumble in serried ridges into Dorset. There is a spacious permanence about this undulating landscape, where fields of feathered barley and pale green waving wheat are interspersed by great swathes of beech-riven chalk upland, pierced only occasionally by tracts of thorn-break and briar.

It is a land of bright harvest-sunshine and magnificent cloud formations. In summer it is shrouded in the rich blue of that *'unattainable flower of the sky',* yet even on the most sultry of days there is always a breeze; and to lie on the springy turf and listen to the rustle the wind makes in the bennet is to imagine that you are hearing the whisper of some far-distant sea-tide. Even when frost holds the land there is still a breeze, but so slight that all is hushed and motionless, save for the hawk that hovers and side-slips and hovers again against a slate-grey sky as it searches for prey. On such winter days as these, clouds scurry across the scene, with here and there a gleam of sunlight to flame a blackened hedgerow amber for a moment and then pass onward to where the sun picks out the tower of a church in silver, or the gabled end of a brick-built cottage in military scarlet. Light and shadow everywhere change and exchange upon the lower chalk slopes of the hills, the evanescent sunshine clarifying small fields without number, whilst into this peace steals the sound of church-bells from distant downland hamlets.

The Chalkland valleys south of Salisbury Plain are rarely more than two miles wide, and nestling in their snug folds are trees of wych-elm and oak among glades of rowan and crab apple. Ash, hazel, hawthorne and sloe stand so thickly in wayside hedges that villages are often almost hidden from sight. Valley floors are a rich alluvial deposit from which the downs rise upwards on either side, supplanting pasture for ploughland as the soils become thinner and the white chalk breaks through. Among the water-meads of the combe, rivulets promote the growth of withy-alder and a carpet of lush green grass (where moorhens make their nests) is spangled and starred in the first freshness of the year by innumerable wild flowers. They come to the very edge of the chalk stream – the little bluebell-like campanula, the squinancywort, the yellow bedstraw, the delicate purple scabious, the lilac-coloured rampion and the creamy-white butterfly orchis.

Topping the scarp of the chalkland district are monuments which point to the vast antiquity of human settlement within this hill-country – an area once the centre of a religion now lost to the knowledge of man. We can only speculate as to the motivating factors which prompted the raising of such incredible monuments as Avebury, Stonehenge and the awesome magnitude of the man-made mound of Silbury Hill. Less spectacular, though no less impressive, works abound in this open countryside – grey wethers and sarsens, dolmen and megaliths stand in fields and on bare downs like human figures frozen for all time, marking the route to Wiltshire's Neolithic cathedrals. From a later era the White Horse of Uffington on the sweeping Berkshire chalk points to the deification of Epona by Iron-Age Celts who cut her sinuous form into the grassy hillside in the centuries predating Christ, when the period of the horse cult first became prominent.

Of a considerably earlier age are the hills themselves; formed during the Cretaceous period. However, unlike the chalkland of Wiltshire and Berkshire, the Chilterns are never referred to as 'downs.' They display much of the downland character but cling to their own rigid identity, the signature of which are their beechwoods – dense, silent places (as only the high woods of the Chilterns can be silent), embowered in 'Gothic' avenues of leaf, branch and sinewed trunk – bathed in the opalescent light invariably associated with the area. In springtime the Chilterns are a sea of bluebells and cherry blossom, and in early summer nightingales may be heard: always there is the smell of beech leaves and cherry wood, and the curl of smoke ascending through trees – the blue smoke of wood fires.

The South East
Weald and Chalk Downland

There is nothing spectacular, there is neither the grandeur of mountains nor the sweep of great rivers to add drama to the aspect of South-East England. It is a land of tranquil beauties; of rolling chalk downland, areas of pine and broad-leaved woodland, greensand hills rich with vegetation, little streams in wooded valleys and agricultural land of many shades – of plough, pasture and orchard. The landscape displays a harmony that is at once varied and homely – almost intimate – and peculiarly English.

The area's many different geological formations compound its diversity and have effect upon both the flora and fauna as well as the distinctive building styles of this south-eastern corner of England. Not the least of its treasures are to be found in architectural features – in the little Saxon and Romanesque churches faced with chalk, tufa and split flint; in the ragstone castles of England's defensive shore, now tinged with the colour of honey by time-encrusted lichens; in Kent's cylindrical oast-houses with their red-slated roofs and wooden wind cowls, used for drying hops; in the whitewashed clapboarding of Tudor farmhouses; and in the mellow timber and brick of 18th century village cottages.

To treat such a varied tract as the four counties of Kent, Sussex, Surrey and Hampshire as one unit is not an easy task, yet all have at least two features in common, which are in fact the South-East's predominant characteristic. Firstly, there are the chalk downlands, the most significant range of southern hills which include the South Downs of Sussex and the long line of the North Downs which rise in Hampshire and traverse Surrey and Kent to end abruptly at Shakespeare's Cliff near Folkestone. These uplands, dappled in spring and summer with moving blue shadow, are bare of foliage where the chalk comes near to the surface, but trees grow in profusion wherever pockets of clay supplant the chalk. Here beech trees predominate, forming clumps, that – like the Chanctonbury Ring and the thickets at Cranborne Chase – are far-seen landmarks invariably cast into prominence by great billowing crowns of shining cloud.

Much of these rolling hills remains unwooded, yet there is compensation in the beauty of springy turf scattered with hairbells and tiny heathers, and spiced with marjoram and wild thyme. It is in remote places such as these – on the wind-swept ridges of South-East England – that plovers wheel above clover-scented turf cropped since time immemorial by great flocks of sheep which find pasture in the downland sheep-walks. Near their summit are trackways worn into existence by the tread of Neolithic man; and along these ancient paths are to be found dolmens, stone circles, flint workings and haunting human imagery – chalk figures incised in the turf – such as the Long Man of Wilmington and the Cerne Abbas Giant – relics of an age when Salisbury Plain was the centre of a civilization which flourished more than four thousand years ago. The very remoteness of such mysterious hill-top places attracted superstition, and local lore states that Woden, one-eyed and wise beyond all knowing, stalks the lonely downs wildly hunting on black and stormy nights for the lost souls of his ancient peoples.

Stretching between the steep escarpment of the North and South Downs lies the area's second notable feature, a wonderful expanse of woodland – much of it a relic of the great British forest of *Andred* – which comprises the Weald of Southern England. Its timber has been stripped for shipbuilding – the navy's *Hearts of Oak* – and for use in the numerous ironworks of Sussex and lowland Kent, evidence of which can be seen in the old hammer ponds which dot the landscape. Surviving areas of the *Andred* tend to be small in extent and consist of ash, hazel, chestnut and the ever-present oak, but what these woodlands lack in scale is more than made up for by their intimate charm – by small brooks that meander through them, and by the carpet of primroses, bluebells and delightful 'wind flowers' (the wood anemone) which yearly show their blooms among the gnarled roots of great trees, struggling through briar growth and blackthorn to herald the advent of spring.

Always there are the Downs on one hand and the fertile expanse of wooded valley on the other, stretching away as far as the eye can see. In summer there is a brilliant colouring in farmland, nestling as it does beneath the chalk uplands and shielded by discreet pockets of coppice woodland. Here the rich tint of poppies growing on the margin of ploughland, in the field hedge, and on the downs themselves bring a splash of scarlet to set off the viridian of distant hills and the flaming-gold of ripening harvest. Indeed, among this lush landscape of abundance with its orchards and pastures, nature seems to speak with the very voice of scripture –

Thou visitest the earth, and waterest it:
Thou greatly enrichest it with the river of God,
Which is full of water: thou preparest them corn,
When thou had so provided for it.
Thou waterest the ridges thereof abundantly:
Thou settlest the furrows thereof:
Thou makest it soft with showers:
Thou blessest the springing thereof.
Thou crownest the year with thy goodness;
And thy paths drop fatness.
They drop upon the pastures of the wilderness:
And the little hills rejoice on every side.
The pastures are clothed with flocks:
The valleys also are covered over with corn:
They shout for joy, they also sing.

The Eastern Counties
The Broads, Brecklands and the Fens

The landscape of East Anglia is typically one of sweeping views, in low relief but by no means flat. It comprises areas of intense contrast: of Fenland, whose dark waters cowl sedge-swamps and reed-beds in shadowed morasses and lagoons; of estuary, mile upon mile of mud flats, and 'meals' – vast salt marshes – a lonely kingdom of wildfowl where wading birds and geese flock in their thousands. The landscape also encompasses the curious peat-dug Broadland where bitterns boom their eerie call – a labyrinth of dykes and half-reclaimed marshes – impenetrable to any but a native; and sandy heath known as Breckland whose abiding primeval spirit is reflected in the gloomy flint-pits of Grime's Graves, quarried locally four thousand years ago. Such features are among the least spoilt of any in Britain, and are experienced to the full in wintertime, when blackened heaths and mist-haunted reed-meres reveal the solitary nature of a land racked by piercing winds driven from the North Sea.

In direct contrast to these desolate spots, the majority of the eastern counties is given over to intensive arable farmland, whose rich dark soils are numbered among the most fertile in the world. Here the landscape is entirely pastural, swelling into gentle golden ridges, the crests of which carry hedgerows, the occasional coppice and farmsteads. This lush countryside of stream-splashed water meadows and fresh valleys has a character very much its own. It is this enchanting aspect of landscape that held one of its most famous sons in awe. For John Constable the calm of his native East Anglia held a particular fascination, *'the beauty of the surrounding scenery,'* he wrote, *'its gentle declivities, the luxuriant meadow flats sprinkled with flocks and herds, its well-cultivated uplands, its woods and rivers with numerous scattered villages and churches, farms and picturesque cottages, all impart to this particular part an elegance hardly anywhere else to be found'.* If 'elegance' has perhaps changed its implication, the scene has altered little since Constable first painted it, and the Stour Valley still expresses, perhaps as completely as anywhere, the spirit of pastoral England at its best.

As with Constable's Suffolk canvases, it is the element of air and towering columns of cloud – an effect heightened by an intense vibration of light created both by the nearness of the sea, and the spread of inland waters – that combine to characterise the unique quality of the East Anglian scene. Contrasting regions as diverse as Fenland and Breck, pasture and Broad, are united under the all-embracing skyscapes of the eastern counties, and each, however different from its neighbour, is evoked by that vista of open, long horizons where heaven and lonely earth seem to mingle and melt into a fusion of misty blue distance.

Throughout East Anglia water dominates the landscape – be it in the mixture of saltings, shingle ridges, sand dunes and marsh of the Norfolk coastline; or the sluggish rivers (some rising only a mile or two from the sea) which form reed-choked meres varying in nature from secluded lakelets to vast expanses, as wide as inland seas; or the fragmented marshes of the Broads, scented with meadow sweet and the sharp tang of water mint. The inconsistencies of tides have silted over harbour mouths, such as Cley, that once dispatched whalers to Iceland, and ships against the Armada. Nowhere, however, does the influence of water prevail and impose itself more upon the landscape than in the Fen country of Cambridgeshire and Lincolnshire, where a million acres of rich agricultural land have been claimed by the drainage of Fenland rivers – the Great Ouse, the Nene, the Wissey and the Welland. Here, almost treeless fields are endlessly intersected by runnels which, although artificial, are in many ways one of the most distinctive features of the landscape. Fenland is a vast flat region – much of it below sea-level – upon which bad weather can induce a depression unprecedented in other surroundings, and the winters bleakness must be experienced through long months to be realised. Yet, for all this, the Fens possess an abiding beauty – not borne of the careless English adornment of hill, stream and meadow, but one in which wide spaces and vast restless skyscapes alter its features with each variation of weather, and demand a tribute to each changing mood.

Fenland, more than other regions, is naturally bound up with its own history. In its original state the area was an overgrown, waterlogged morass – in winter an inland sea, and in summer a swamp of stagnant meres, teeming with fish and fowl. Its few inhabitants lived on the remote patches of firm ground that stood out like islands above a clouded sea: little wonder, therefore, that this traditional haunt of lost causes should attract the sterner monastic Orders to these remote island sites far removed from the turbulence of medieval life. Here they gradually transformed the fen into scattered settlements – green oases about their mighty churches. Such were Thorney, Ramsey, Chatteris and Crowland – whose shattered fragments of abbeys remain – yet greatest of all, in extent and importance, is the Isle of Ely, where the Norman Minster still stands out defiantly against the violet light of the endless flats of the Great Level – the medieval flower of the surrounding domain it had conquered.

The West Midland Vales
The Cotswolds and Malvern Hills

The rolling countryside of the West-Midland Vales – a landscape of elm-fringed water meadows of the Severn and Avon, and orchards laden with damson, cherry, apple and pear – is the green heartland of England. It is the misty-green vale from which Elgar drew his music and, centuries beforehand, Langland had his vision of Piers Plowman. At its centre is the Vale of Evesham, perhaps the most productive fruit-growing district in all Britain. The land is naturally at its most beautiful at Eastertide when its orchards are enveloped in a white foam of blossom: in pockets of wayside vegetation bluebells are found in such profusion that coppice-margins and hedgebanks are *'washed wet like lakes'* – bathed in pools of light – whose sheen continually changes as the drooping flower-heads swirl to heavily-scented breezes.

The quiet capital of its own vale, the town of Evesham arose round an abbey of which only the bell tower now survives. As with the landscape's other ecclesiastical glories, notably the medieval abbey at Tewkesbury and the cathedral towers of Gloucester and Worcester, form and construction have been meticulously honed to complement the surrounding countryside's unique qualities of light – an effect best observed (in the alliterative words of Langland's poetry), *'In somer season when soft is the sonne.'* Indeed, it is this element of luminosity – of gathering light – that best characterises the jagged Malvern Hills to the west, and illuminates the gentle, bow-headed, 'whale-back' landscape of the Cotswolds which stretch beyond the vale to south and to east.

It is here in the wold, with its predominance of honey-brown masonry, that the stones themselves appear to glow. When the limestone is first quarried it is a bleached grey, yet with the mellowing influence of time, cottages, barns and dry stone walling blush a tawny hue and acquire a radiance that marvellously merges the work of man with the spacious beauties of the surrounding hills. These are the elements that go to produce the Cotswold picture. It is a vision of undulating hillsides heaving buff-green into the distance, their thin fringes of scattered beech clear-cut against a crowded sky. It is the seclusion of valleys, lined with pollard willows, along which a clear brook threads its silver course – a haunt of lazy, dappled trout and gadding mayfly. It is a land of expansive pastures dotted with cowslip, orchis, celandine, scabious and buglewort; of hedgeside daisies; and fallow fields that sweep the brow of the wold and then fall to the vale below. There are few villages to be seen; only now and then in the distance comes a hamlet, caught in a fold of hills, whose gabled stone houses with weathered stone-slate roofs reflect the sun amongst the green of moss and the yellow of lichens.

Cotswold villages are invariably strung along the course of a stream: the Windrush, the Coln, or the Evenlode, to name but a few, and each displays a careful craftsmanship and sense of style that is the particular achievement of the district. The 'Cotswold style' has remained a constant expression of local materials and need; it had its birth towards the close of the 14th century; certainly by the 15th century it had reached a high degree of maturity – as expressed by buildings such as Icomb Manor and those in the High Street at Chipping Campden. However, it is the smaller manor houses at Owlpen, Upper Slaughter, Upper Swell and Snowhill that epitomise the dignified Cotswold expression of pride in local prosperity and achievement.

A word must also be said for the churches. It is remarkable how many of these remain the primitive little structures that were raised almost a thousand years ago when the manors of the wold were first parcelled out among the Norman Lords. Though externally some of them might well belong to any medieval epoch, several (most notably at Elkstone and Hampnett) can reveal perfect Romanesque interiors hardly touched by the hand of time. The beginnings of prosperity in the 13th century – when the Cotswolds were the heart of England's wool industry – is reflected in an Early English group as typical as any in the country; North Cerney and Duntisbourne being particularly attractive, with their saddleback towers. The glory of the district is, however, the later 'wool churches' that, collectively, remain as grand a memorial to the munificence of their merchant patrons as to the genius of the masons who evoked such splendours from the resources of locally quarried limestone. Fabrics such as the Northleach, Fairford, Cirencester, Campden and Winchcombe parish churches rank with any in the land for their beauty of craftsmanship.

The Welsh Borderland
The Marcher Hills and Valleys

The countryside of the Welsh Borderland is possessed of a power and impressiveness – and elegance of spirit – that rivals anything that the rest of Britain can offer. Here a variety of elements, of river and dell, of orchard and swelling pasture, of woodland and hedgerow-patterned fields, mingle in a tangled complex of steep valleys and hills to produce an ensemble of sweetness and beauty.

A rural peace reigns over this landscape which spreads upwards from valley floors to the curving crests of the ridge and then drops again through skirting woods to where little rills curl among their water-meads. Seasonal colouring is everywhere apparent; in the greens and russet of bracken, in the black and purple of heather, and in the rain-soaked verdure of bent and bilberry. On a windy day it is an invigorating experience to follow the turf tracks that run along the Marcher crests; looking westwards into the wind to view the darkened, bold moorland summits, and beyond them to the azure outline of more hills (pierced occasionally by splashes of purple ploughland) and yet more ridges, backed by the profiles of the Welsh peaks. In the opposite direction lies the almost limitless expanse of the Midland Plain, heaving mile upon mile into a far distant haze. It is a prospect beloved of John Masefield, who knew well its moods and subtleties,

"I have seen dawn and sunset on moor and windy hills coming in solemn beauty . . ."

The Marcher region lies between the two great estuaries of Dee and Severn and extends southwards from Chester through the vale country of Cheshire and Shropshire (the hills and finger-ridges of the south part of that county), the tumbled plain of Herefordshire and the uplands of Monmouthshire and Dean. Along its line rise the high hills of Wales, massed in close formation – sometimes sending spurs into English soil, sometimes parting to admit green tongues of farmland into valleys threaded by swift rivers. There is a wild beauty in these vales, with their small, white, half-timbered farmhouses in magpie garb, and tumbled woods dwarfed by the austere sweeps of the heights above. Through this land from north to south the old Borderline wavers, often with an arbitrary parting of neighbouring hills, but still largely following the direction of the turf breastwork built in the 8th century by the Mercian, King Offa.

The Welsh Borderland is a landscape of contrast – upland, rock formations, mountains such as the Wrekin in the west, and rich dairy pastures and grasslands to the north. At Ludlow, for example, can be seen a complete English composition with all the traditional features of harvest cornfields and a predominance of stately trees – oak, fir and beech. In contrast, the Stiperstones are sharp and bare with tor-like outcrops of dark rock – the haunt of kestrel and raven – or beyond to the singularly graceful peak of Corndon Hill facing sheer across country to the hedge-patterned mass of the Long Mountain and the copious triple summit of the Breidden hills.

Apart from intrinsic beauty, the Welsh Marches hold a history steeped in romance. The memory of early struggles is handed down in mighty earth-fastnesses – Croft Ambrey, Wapley, Nordy Bank – and in the husks of ruined castles such as Wigmore, Clun, Ludlow and Hopton, which stand as mute witness to centuries of turmoil and violence that abated only after the Civil War.

The subjugation of Wales was a task too formidable for direct under-taking, even by the Normans, so it came about that the Borderlands were divided out amongst the more enterprising of their soldier-adventurers who were given *carte-blanche* to build themselves fortifications from which they could conquer the wild and scattered native population. The new rulers established themselves by force and existed in watchful defence within the confines of their so-called Lordship Marchers. Nevertheless, in the majority of cases their rule was equable so that before long townships and villages grew up beneath Norman keeps: such were Wigmore, Hay, Montgomery, Clun and scores more – quiet places nowadays that seem to belong to their past, half asleep in the shadows of their castle crags. Thus, through the great medieval upheavals – the crumbling of the Llewellyn Princes, the encroachment of Marcher fiefs, the campaigning of the Plantagenets, and the culminating tragedy of Owain Glyndŵr – has this wild and once remote landscape been transformed into a tract of some of the quietest and most lovely of Country Shires.

Wales *The Spirit and the Face*

Wales is an extraordinary mixture of the obvious and the recondite, a country of romantic legends and ruined castles, yet the overpowering spirit of the landscape is one of Gothic drama – a wild mountainous terrain of vast, indigo, cloud-misted distances, pervaded by the sound of sweet water and birdsong. Here is a depth of vision leading you into the centre of an almost untouchable world of clear light and exhilarating vista – a land where curlews flock in their thousands to feed upon damp moorland, their wild plaint, at first joyous and then of long despairing lament, seems to haunt Wales eternally.

In the days of the Princes, Wales was always regarded as three entities, the Northern Kingdom of Gwynedd, The Middle Kingdom of Powis, and the Southern Kingdom of Deheubarth. Powis was never a very strong power and seldom stood by its own might; nowadays it is only a vague historical memory. Not so, however, the other two. Wales is only a unified country in the mind of the idealist – in practice it is divided into North and South. The division is precise and occurs at the River Dovey; this point is a boundary not only of Welsh feeling – between the Anglicized lands of South Wales, and the spirit of Celtic individualism which has been the hallmark of the Northern lands since the 13th century – but scenery also, the sharp mountains of the Cambrian Range lying to the north of the Dovey, whilst smoother, less dramatic mountains spread southwards across the Deheubarth landscape.

In Southern Wales history delivered a hammerblow to Welsh nationhood by the gradual inroads made by Norman Marcher Lords who extended English conquest from the mouth of the Wye as far west as Pembrokeshire's Atlantic headland. Along this fief, part of which is still referred to as 'Little England beyond Wales', are found the ruins of the most impressive castles in Wales – Caerphilly. Manorbier, Carew, Chepstow and Llanstephan, with a host more on a lesser scale of grandeur. Everywhere along this feudal tract the Norman and English cultures dominate – fine stone houses were constructed; magnificent churches were raised; and towns on the old English plan were built.

As the south coast of Wales has its line of castles stretching from the Marches to the ocean boundary, so has the Welsh northern seaboard a string of impregnable fortresses at Conway, Beaumaris, Rhuddlan, Caernarvon and Harlech – but these are of quite a different order. The former were as much baronial mansions as fortresses, whilst the latter, built by King Edward I after his conquest of Wales, were just fortified barracks for royal troops. The countryside around these bastions showed no signs of a spread of English culture and remains today as Welsh in speech, feeling and lack of architectural impulse as it ever was.

Under the yoke of Plantagenet kings the flower of Celtic independence retreated into the fastness of the Snowdonia landscape – vast mountains, notched in places like battlemented towers, with high passes and craggy peaks – from where the spirit of Welsh freedom occasionally resurfaced in the guise of her hero princes – Llywelyn the Great, Llywelyn ap Gruffydd and Owain Glyndŵr. Some part of this essence of defiance seems to linger in these wild, northern mountains to haunt this highland of rock and heather where nothing appears to have altered since the Ice Age; all is embraced by silence, save for the bleat of lambs, the sudden flight of snipe, or the solitary call of the rare red kite – described by one native poet as *'the living flame of the sky.'* Here are great sweeping moorlands, rising to mountainous masses 2,000 feet or more in height and interspersed with marsh-flats ablaze with golden gorse flower. Views are wide and horizons far: the wind sweeps freely across the vastness, and the skylark and meadow pipit's song is lost to the breeze. However, soaring above all – dominating all – is the ethereal azure mass of Snowdon – the focus of bardic song and sentiment throughout the ages.

North Wales is a land composed almost entirely of ancient rock formations whose contorted form and denuded surfaces were produced by ice pressure millions of years ago. In the great mass of the northern Cambrian Range, Snowdon at 3,500 feet, Carnedd Dafydd at 3,426 feet, and Carnedd Llywelyn at 3,484 feet, are sister peaks – barren on their upper slopes and in winter season snow covered – their summits reflected in lonely blue and black lakes of crystal purity set high up in their mountain folds. South and East of Snowdon, on the 2,000 feet contour, are the Arenig moorlands, the Berwyn Mountains and the Harlech Dome. These, in turn, are skirted by a rolling landscape intersected by moor and patches of peat-mire, which are almost intimidating in their sense of splendid immunity from traces of human activity – all, that is, except for an occasional ruined stone and slate cottage, the long deserted shelter of shepherds seeking the high summer pastures.

The central plateau melts into Mid-Wales, and the Plynlimon group whose characteristics are rounded grassy shapes, worn into innumerable furrows, culminating in one very definite mountain – Plynlimon. Although in height it only rises 2,465 feet, there is something very grand and distinctive about it. Plynlimon represents the corner stone of all three provinces of Medieval Wales, and also, in the peat bogs of its slopes, gives birth to both the Severn and the Wye.

Further south, along the Cambrian backbone of Wales, lie the contorted hills, tall shadowy rock gorges and great cascades of foaming water that form the Brecon Beacons. They rise to 2,906 feet at Pen y Fan and are named from their use as sites for signal fires. The wind-lashed summits have a dragonlike outline, sporting sheer precipices which fall 600 feet and have been likened to the crests of giant waves about to break into the deep valley gorges, or 'cwns,' below. On either side of the Beacons are the East and West Black Mountains. They have very distinctive individualities, and it is unfortunate and confusing that they should share a similar name – even the colour is wrong, for they are composed of outcrops of red Devonian sandstone. The Eastern group – marking the end of Wales, and the beginning of England – are imposing whale-backed barriers holding a series of long valleys, all 'blind' at the northern end. In one of these cwns is situated the beautiful, lonely ruin of Llanthony Abbey, whose monks deserted it as early as the 12th century. It was abandoned during the lawless reign of Stephen, yet to stand on its site and feel the mountains enclosing around, one wonders if it was not the overpowering nature of the savage scenery that overawed the brethren rather than the turmoil of marcher wars.

Middle England
Shire Country of Hedge and Pasture

One of the proudest titles attached to any area of England is 'The Shires.' This heavy, fertile land, with its flat fields and massive hedgerows, well grown elms, grazing cattle and trim farms, encompasses the counties of Middle England – notably, Leicestershire, Huntingdonshire, Staffordshire, Warwickshire, Northamptonshire and the ancient county of Rutland – their wold and fen; slow meandering rivers and gentle undulating countryside earning for the Shires the accolade of being considered the 'true' English Landscape – a homely attraction not easily paralleled in other lands, in other counties.

The enfolded fields of Middle England, their pastures enclosed by blackthorn and quick-set hedges, resemble nothing so much as a vast patchwork of landscape – a series of green meadows; golden in the aftermath of harvest; or brown, fawn and ochre where ploughed land has not yet yielded a crop. This is the traditional home of the grazier and the huntsman. The firm, sweet grass is widely spread and stock fatten on it and flourish as they do in few other places. Over these rich feeding grounds ride Britain's premier Hunts, the famous Belvoir (named from the ancestral seat of the Dukes of Rutland), the Pytchley and the Quorn. Indeed, the landscape might have been purposely laid out for hunting; even the woods seem tamed, used as fox coverts. The meads of this gently rolling clay country are punctuated by ash trees, put in as standards, and the majority of hedges date back to the Enclosure Acts of the Georgian Period when thorn was inevitably used for making a fast-growing hedgerow. They offer excellent jumping and all are wide enough to hide a fox at its last gasp.

Most of the great Hunts exult in grass, as does the dairy farmer, but where Middle England begins, so to speak, on the east, and the clay slopes rise from the peat of the Fens, the countryside, although rather heavy and flat, is first-class wheat and bean land. The latter crop has a singular association with the Midland landscape (somewhat similar to that of the hop with Kent) which makes the crimson flower of the runner bean a predominant colour in high-summer, splashing the astonishing brightness of its bloom upon both farmland, where it bines along canes, and village and hamlet where it outshines even the traditional cottage-garden flowers of stock, pansy and rose. The Northamptonshire poet John Clare held its beauties in high regard:

A Beanfield full in blossom smells as sweet
As Araby, or groves of orange flowers;
Black-eyed and white, and feathered to one's feet,
How sweet they smell in morning's dewy hours!
When seething night is left upon the flowers,
And when morn's sun shines brightly o'er the field,
The bean-bloom glitters in the gems of showers,
And sweet the fragrance which the union yields
To battered footpaths crossing o'er the fields.

As with the beauty to be found in the summer abundance of bean flowers, so is the landscape of the Shires best exemplified by the intimacy of its most common features. The true glory of England is its hedgerows, and nowhere is this more apparent than in Middle England. From the day when first commons and common-fields were enclosed, quick-hedges were planted. The slips were cut from hawthorn bushes that had always dotted the country and made breaks. These quicks set beside ditches – by reputation a yard deep and four feet across – grew like weeds and made the glorious paddocks and pastures that pattern the green mosaic that is today the surface of England. Within these hedgerows – now composed of holly, elder, hedge maple, crab apple and the ubiquitous hawthorn – are to be glimpsed the intimate treasures of the Shires.

At no other time of year are these 'glimpses' lovelier than at springtide when dripping hedgebanks and rain soaked fields are russet-brown or smokey-purple according to the play of sunlight upon the scene. The landscape is still a winter one, only flushed with spring at intervals, but birth is an imperceptible thing in nature; growth emerges quickly and suddenly in colours of misty green and grey. Its silent impetus is wonderfully evoked by Clare, writing of his native countryside:

'The dewdrops on every blade of grass are so much like silver drops that I am
obliged to stoop down as I walk to see if they are pearls, and those sprinkled
on the ivy-woven beds of primroses underneath the hazels, whitethorns, and
maples are so like gold beads that I stooped down to feel if they were hard, but
they melted from my finger. And where the dew lies on the primrose, the violet
and whitethorn leaves, they are emerald and beryl, yet nothing more than the
dews of the morning on the budding leaves; nay, the road grasses are covered
with gold and silver beads, and the further we go the brighter they seem to

shine, like solid gold and silver. It is nothing more than the sun's light and shade upon them in the dewy morning; every thorn-point and every bramble-spear has its trembling ornament: till the wind gets a little brisker, and then all is shaken off, and all the shining jewelry passes away into a common spring morning full of budding leaves, primroses, violets, vernal speedwell, bluebell and orchis and commonplace objects.

Thus were the Shire hedgerows planted, from necessity and by law, yet they have become beautiful in themselves. The oaks, ash, sycamores and elms which form the hedge standards are perhaps the most important growths in the whole landscape of these Isles.

The North Country
Moorland, Dales and Wold

Yorkshire, Northumberland and Durham were once part of the great Saxon Kingdom of Northumbria, and these wild, often windswept counties share a history as turbulent as any in Britain. In the days before industrialism laid wide-grasping hands upon the valleys and rivers, there was scarcely a square mile of land lying between the waters of Trent and Tweed which had not some charm and beauty to reveal. But when the demand for iron-ore and coal increased as manufacturing developed, stretches of a hitherto solitary land became utterly changed in aspect and character. Fortunately the major part of the Northern landscape remains unscarred and still forms one of the largest tracts of unspoilt countryside in England.

The wolds of the East Riding, North Riding and Lincolnshire are still given over to solitude – wherein the only tenants are cattle and shaggy Swaledale sheep – and their vast distances and lonely horizons remain much as Tennyson described them,

> *'Calm and deep peace of this high wold,*
> *And on these dews that drench the furze'.*

The Peak country of Derbyshire is still an expanse of loveliness; and the great Yorkshire Dales remain unspoilt, their scattered, whitewashed farmsteads, dale villages and hamlets – a few cottages grouped together in a huddle of stunted trees, set far enough apart to give each an aspect of seclusion – are yet as Wordsworth knew them, lying deep and low at the foot of the high fells, each *beneath its little patch of sky, and little lot of stars'.* Solitude, isolation from the world of industry, which is, after all, so near – these are still the prevalent characteristics of the northern dales and wolds.

Moorland, like mountain, is one of the permanencies of landscape, and has been called the 'last English wilderness'. Such a description is particularly worthy of the high, cold countryside of the Yorkshire moors and those of Durham and Northumberland, whose wide, open vistas and immense, birdswept skies are the hunting-ground of *'dapple-dawn-drawn'* falcons – the noble *'windhovers'* of the rolling plain. In summer,

when moorlands 'blow' with the flowers of wild eglantine and hairbells, the prevailing colour of the land is stained with the purple of heather and the yellow of vast swags of gorse and broom; yet in winter's grip – if the moors have not become interfolding acres of drifting snow and hazy blue shadow – the colour of the landscape takes on a sinister hue – reflecting the predominant granite rocks in bleak greyness, or in the browns of dead bracken. Probably the best known northern moors are those of the West Riding – at Keighley and Wadsworth – because of their nearness to the Brontë family home at Haworth. A lane near the Parsonage leads out onto the moorland, where, in the stark winter weather of 1848, Charlotte set out in search of a sprig of heather, thinking it might revive her dying sister Emily. The spirit of these wild places is sombre; leaden clouds suppress the landscape, and dry-stone walling which patterns the valleys shows grey in the sunlight, and black in rain – yet under such dark cloud the moor itself turns a deep green beneath the stillness of heather and gorse.

The Pennines stretch from Derbyshire to the farthermost parts of Northumberland and offer some of England's finest walking country. Huge expanses of upland moor – looking much as they have done since the beginning of history – sweep to a score of summits of more than 2,000 feet in the Yorkshire Dales. Over a million years ago, ice flowing down the eastward tilt of the Pennine watershed carved out the dales in their distinctive shapes. Wensleydale, watered by the River Ure, with its ravines and spectacular waterfalls of Hardraw Force and the cataracts of Aysgarth, is the broadest, most open and well-forested of the Yorkshire valleys, where tree, rock and river combine to make a prospect of rare charm. Swaledale, its sudden twists and sinuous windings beneath its steep hills, has a more secluded grandeur, and narrower, tributary dales, such as Arkengarthdale, Bishopdale and Coverdale burrow deep between the flanks of the fells. These hills are of limestone, capped here and there by millstone grit, and upon them grow cotton grass and heather, flecked with bilberry and crowberry. There is also softer natural beauty among the rugged landscape – in the treasury of Alpine flowers left behind by the Ice Age around Teesdalehead in Durham; and in the valleys are the remains of monastic buildings that are scattered all over the North East. Yorkshire's Fountains Abbey, founded in 1132, is the best known; Bolton Priory ('Abbey' as it is locally, but erroneously, called) set in a wooded gorge besides the River Wharfe; and Rievaulx Abbey, which is perhaps the most romantically sited of all.

In Northumberland the Pennines merge imperceptibly with the Cheviot Hills – its moors and dales – whose remote summits command inspiring views of the Tweed gliding away to Berwick and the far sea; and beyond the river, the smiling, placid acres of the Scottish Lowlands. Walter Scott wrote of this landscape: *'The Cheviots were before me in frowning majesty; not indeed with the smiling majesty of rock and cliff which characterises mountains of the primary class, but huge round-headed and cloathed with a dark robe of russet, gaining by their extent and desolate appearance an influence upon the imagination, as a desert district possessing a character of its own'.* In the past these solitary hills were the scene of much border dispute and bloodshed, made famous in ballads such as 'Chevy Chase' which celebrates the battle between the armies of Earl Douglas and the Percys of Northumberland. These hills, which once resounded to the clash of sword and claymore in the fierce hand-to-hand fighting of the Border Wars, now echo only to the cry of the curlew. Amid the Cheviots' magnificent scenery – where star saxifrage and spring gentians are still to be found – rise the bold domes of the hills, riding across the border like massive waves.

The North West
Lakeland, Mountain and Fell

Cumbria, land of misty mountains and placid lakes, has a landscape of dramatic light and shade which possesses all the grandeur and concentrated beauty of configuration that one usually associates with the Alps. English Lakeland, with its sweeping fells and dales, is probably the most definitely bounded of all Britain's regions – lying between the massive divide of the Pennine highlands on the east and the sea-coast on the west; to the north stretches the wide spread of the Solway Firth, whilst the silver tidal-flats of Morecombe Bay denote its southern limit. In past ages the land was densely wooded, and was so remote from the rest of England that Cumbria was looked upon as a natural part of Scotland until late Norman times. The Rey stone on Stainmoor was then regarded as the boundary marker between English and Scottish thrones – as it still is the marker between Cumbria and the rest of England.

Such rugged terrain remained empty, or nearly so, until it was populated by the last of the great migrations into Britain due to the wanderings and settlements of the Vikings, which took them to Iceland, Greenland and even to the seaboard of Newfoundland; and in Britain, to the occupation of Shetland, the Orkneys, the Isle of Man and much of Western Scotland. In the 10th century they took possession of this land of purple mountains and lakes of inky-blackness, whose desolation must have appeared to them out of the mists, out of the rain, in all its ancient terror. However, the Norsemen stamped their indelible mark upon what is now called the 'Lake District' and nearly all the place names of Cumberland and Westmorland are of their tongue – '*dale*' and '*fell*', '*force*' (a waterfall), '*thwaite*' (cleared ground), and '*tarn*' from the nordic word '*tiorn*' (a tear). The Vikings are also responsible for the most fascinating relics of the district – the crosses of Gosforth and Bewcastle. The former displays a strange mixture of pagan myth and Christian symbolism, whilst the latter cross is incised in the tradition of Byzantine craft with a strength of design and power of execution that points to close links between their lakeside settlements and the distant Bosphorus, perhaps by the Viking trade routes to the Black Sea and Russia.

The region of high, windswept fells, rock crags and distant views of lofty, broken peaks, centres around the mountainous mass that culmi-nates in Scafell and Scafell Pike – which at 3,210 feet is the loftiest peak in England. These are the spectacular images of Wordsworth's poetry:

'The mountains against heaven's grave weight
Rise up, and grow to wondrous height'.

Geographically the area is the domed uplift of the earth's crust, formed by volcanic activity, which has exposed the oldest and hardest rocks at its centre – from where running water has cut dales which radiate like spokes from a wheel from the mountain knot of the Scafell crests. Later, the weight of the Ice Age worked its effect upon the landscape we know today. Sheeted thick with glaciers, the slow movement of ice cut into the valley floors, and when the warmer ages came there were deeply gouged hollows and valleys – dammed by glacial debris – into which the melting waters flowed. Here the grandeur of mountains and the bold austerity of rock crags are mirrored in the still waters of the area's myriad lakes. Among the most notable of these lakes are the lovely Ennerdale Water, Buttermere, Crummock Water, Windermere and Derwent Water – each fed by the crystal streams and rivers of this, the rainiest region in England. Their surface is of an exquisite, piercing turquoise that is not a reflection of the sky, although it may be enhanced by it just as it is changed and patterned by every breath of wind. With the wild scent of bracken and the distant whisperings of waves lapping against reeds, the English Lakes possess a calm serenity. It is the secret haunt of the Lakeland spirit – a landscape of poetic intensity – of ice-blue waters that lie placid among the heights:

'Nought wakens or disturbs their tranquil tides,
Nought but the char that for the may-fly leaps,
And breaks the mirror of the circling deep.'

The most spectacular of the Lakes is also the deepest. Wast Water lies like a stretched silken cloth, scarcely wrinkled in the shadow of Great Gable and The Screes. With volcanic rock and sculptured, marble-like cliffs gathered on all sides, Wast Water comes closer than any other to the primitive state of glacial mere. Its waters are so exceptionally pure that it supports little wildlife – save for char, minnows and sticklebacks.

Lowland Scotland
The Borders and the Uplands

Traditionally, the southern half of Scotland is known as the Lowlands – a description which might suggest flatness and a certain lack of variety, yet nothing could be further from the truth. The Lowlands – a tableland of grassy hills and cool green pastures – stand in dignity, possessing a loveliness that is apt to be overlooked in comparison with the more dramatic splendours that the rugged North-western Highlands can provide. The midland valley between the Forth and the Clyde (the region's uppermost extent) is the only lowland area in the literal sense of the word; and the southern uplands rise to the Tweedsmuir Hills in the centre and the Lammermuir and Pentland Hills in the north-east. Indeed, the Scottish Lowlands are more hilly than most parts of England, and the climate, particularly in the central areas, can be as harsh in mid-winter – when the first flurries of snow come scudding over the summits – as that endured by any lonely hamlet in the Highland mountains.

As always in Scotland, the most dramatic landscapes are to be found where there are hills of size; and each has its own descriptive name: 'dods' are rounded summits; 'laws' are conical hills, and 'rigs' are ridges. Of the Lowland type, the most perfect specimens are to be found in the district where the Solway flats climb northwards over the watershed into Lanarkshire and the valley of the Clyde. These are not the fearsome hills of continual rock outcrop that give the mountains of the west and north their terrifying character, but gentle and wooded for the most part – where conifers and patches of green fields lie in the strath, ascending through skirting mists to where the grey mares' tails of mountain water-falls send their drifts of spray among moss and rock-clinging fern.

The hills rise out of flat farming land, climbing among forests until, imperceptibly, the farmsteads become smaller, the rivers dwindle to brown streams, and growing crops give place to smooth, bronze-green hillsides, marked here and there with a fan of scree thrown out by an occasional winter torrent. Then the deciduous trees disappear and in their stead are found an occasional clump of fir or a plantation of spruce, and little burns run through deep ditches cut in the soft peat. As the air grows colder and the gradient finally eases, you can see mile upon mile of moorland, of which the feature is mainly its curious straw-brown colour, with a tarn here and there reflecting whatever colouring may be in the sky, and all the while, the cries of peesweeps and lambs emphasise the loneliness. In the far distance the landscape mingles with the ocean, and the words of Wordsworth seem to carry in the still air:

> . . . a silver current flows
> With uncontrolled meanderings;
> Nor have these eyes by greener hills
> Been soothed in all my wanderings.

Where the Lowlands run into the sea there are high cliffs and remote beaches of white sand; endless vistas of foam-flecked tides reveal at the foot of every other cleft in the sea-cliff a fine old fishing village with woods about it that might have been lifted directly from remote East Anglia or the coastline of Friesland. It may be a place as big as Eyemouth – large enough to lose a score of able-bodied men in one night of storm – or it might be small and quaint and a trifle bleak like St Abb's, perched on a promontory overlooking a harbour continually assailed by waves. It may be snug and pretty like Burnmouth, or large like Dunbar: yet these fishing communities run to type – and that a rather distinguished type – born of the constant battle between fishermen and the treacherous ocean with its fanged reefs, cross currents and sudden violent storms.

A paradox of Scotland is that these harsh coasts are backed by agricul-tural land of a particularly rich quality. The fields run back from the edge of the cliffs to the hills, green and fruitful; the traditional white walls of the Scots farmsteads making delicious splashes against the monotone of pasture and land under plough. There are not many red roofs in Scotland; the common blue slate covers most of even the rural roofs, but their sombre gleaming above whitewash can make lovely effects against slopes that rise from the ploughed red soil, to where black-faced sheep and wild red deer crop the hard, thin grass of the upland, and where the golden eagle soars overhead.

In this peaceful landscape there are scars of a turbulent past; in the magnificent ruins of castles – Tantallon, Slains and Dunnottar – each overhanging the sea from its rocky crag; and in the gutted remains of great abbeys – Kelso, Jedburgh and Dryburgh – laid to waste by English invaders from the 13th to the 17th centuries. The English, however, were not the only despoilers, for there was dark treachery even among their own kind – notably by the Border reivers, or mosstroopers, and the powerful Border Earls. Wars and feuds, abduction and murder were commonplace, and 'cattle-lifters' raided to the very gates of Edinburgh, showing their contempt for royal authority. Yet out of these deeds come the tales of the 'makkars' — the poets and the 'makers' of ballads. Their stories of love and of war, often laced with sardonic wit, were told in broad Scots. In the hands of the makkars – as in those of Robert Burns – this deceptively harsh language can become a tool of great beauty.

The Highlands
Mountains, Lochs and Islands

The Scottish Highlands possess the most magical and yet the most terri-fying landscape in Britain. Coming up country from the border, through agricultural land full of grey stone and rounded hills, dotted with vestiges of medievalism – ruined castles and bare skeletons of broken abbeys – you see the jagged frieze of the Grampians (the highest and largest mountainous mass in Britain) rise above the northern horizon, blue and dramatic and unmistakable. Their capacity – perhaps an effect of atmospherics – to take on at a distance a wistful, cerulean blue, characterizes all the great mountain ranges of the Scottish Highlands – the Monadhliaths, the Trossachs, the Cairngorms of the Central Heights, and the isolated mountains of the far north. These awesome ranges share the landscape with wild sea lochs that gouge deeply into the land; with icy streams that tumble through green and wooded glens; with frowning crags and darkly shadowed passes; with the calm waters of vast inland lochs and kyles; and, above all, with an ever changing sky that gives rise to an immense variety of shade and subtle hue.

Perhaps the almost excessive popularity of the Highlands is a lingering remnant of Victorian sentiment. It was certainly popularised in the minds of the public by Queen Victoria's affection for similar scenes of Deeside and the general acceptance of that romantic spirit so well encompassed by the nickname 'Balmorality'. To take this combination of pretty images; of conifers, rivers and lakes as a complete representation of the Highlands is to miss beauty infinitely more austere, profound and elusive. Indeed, it does not take any Scottish byway long to rise out of its glen to the high countryside of the mountains – through woods that degenerate into clumps of birch and hazel growing on land that hardens with every hundred feet of altitude gained, until there is only bare rock and moorland scrub. It is not a comfortable scene that meets the wayfarer's eye – but one to marvel at in all its gaunt and threatening majesty. Here is a landscape which changes from green to the brown of peat moors and the silver dazzle of spasmodic torrents fashioned fantastically by the volcanic and glacial crises of the distant past. It seems a cold and lonely place, snow-laden in the dead of winter and often assailed by driving rain; yet beauty, when it is found is – perhaps in the play of cloud-shadows on the bare, bronzed slopes, or the trail of mist across the rocky face of mountains – by its unsuspected nature, all the more enchanting.

Although splendid desolation is now the motif of the Central Highlands – given over to the raven and the deer – it is as well to remember that the countryside was once the home of crofters who contrived to eke out a living from the bleak surroundings: and it is here that clansmen defended these grim passes to the point of death. At Dalwhinnie in the valley of the swift Spey the clans of old gathered in warlike array. Here they repulsed Cromwell in his day, and, more than a century later, the Hanoverian army of General Cope. Further down the glen, near Kingussie, Ruthven Barracks were built in 1718 to keep the Highlands in check, but Bonnie Prince Charlie's Jacobite rebels destroyed them in 1746. The present desolation of these uplands is largely the result of the collapse of his cause and its ultimate destruction on Culloden Moor (surely the most drear and melancholy of all Scottish battlefields). In reprisal, crofters were forcibly evicted from their farmsteads by English troops carrying out their commission against the King's enemies. Every corner of the Highlands seems to have its touching reminder of the troubles – a ruined croft or crumbling barn – recalling the savage depopulation of the 18th and 19th centuries, when the ancestral homeland of its Celtic inhabitants was 'cleared' to make room for large scale sheep farming and English Baronial estates.

The tremendous mountain masses of the Central Heights, however imposing, are at certain seasons so hostile, so acid in colour, that their wilderness depresses rather than exalts the spirit. But towards the west the softer, more poetic light of a moister, warmer climate informs scenes of picturesque splendour with a strange and irrepressible charm. Here are found the main elements – mountains, lochs and islands – in the triumphant chord of Highland beauty. A glance at the map of Scotland reveals how fresh water lochs endlessly stud the region, and how fantastically the western coastline is indented by the sea. Here, tortuous fjords add to the scenic effect, allowing the mysteries of the oceans to send their groping fingers amid the mountains, and to fumble among the tangles of golden weed that line its shores. Near at hand the water is vivid blue, paling into a white brilliance when a burst of sunlight from the sombre sky dazzles the surface, contrasting with the green of its low isles, and, in mid-summer, the yellow of cut hayfields on the far shore. Indeed, on the raw rock of mountain and on the white sands of the tideline, on pasture and on moor, the light cast by the sky and reflected by the sea plays amazing tricks of colour. In storm and in calm it combines in a thousand different ways to present to the seeing eye all the essences of Highland landscape – be it in the violet shades of distant peaks, or in the warm indigo sheen which falls upon fishing villages such as Crail, in Fife. Even Bothwell Castle in Lanarkshire has a pink wash of light at some times of day. How bathed in such light stands Iona, from where Columba started his mission and where his cathedral now abuts the western surf. Deep-cut shadows haunt the memory of Glencoe, darken the Achnashallach Forest, and fall gently across the ruins of Melrose Abbey – reputed to hold the heart of Robert the Bruce.

Facing page: beached fishing boats at Cadgwith, and (overleaf left) the attractive Cornish resort town of St Mawes.

Cornwall. Previous page and facing page: Polperro, one of the county's most delightful villages with its steep, narrow streets and great character. Above: Newlyn Harbour. Overleaf: two views of the spectacularly-rugged cliffs around Land's End.

24

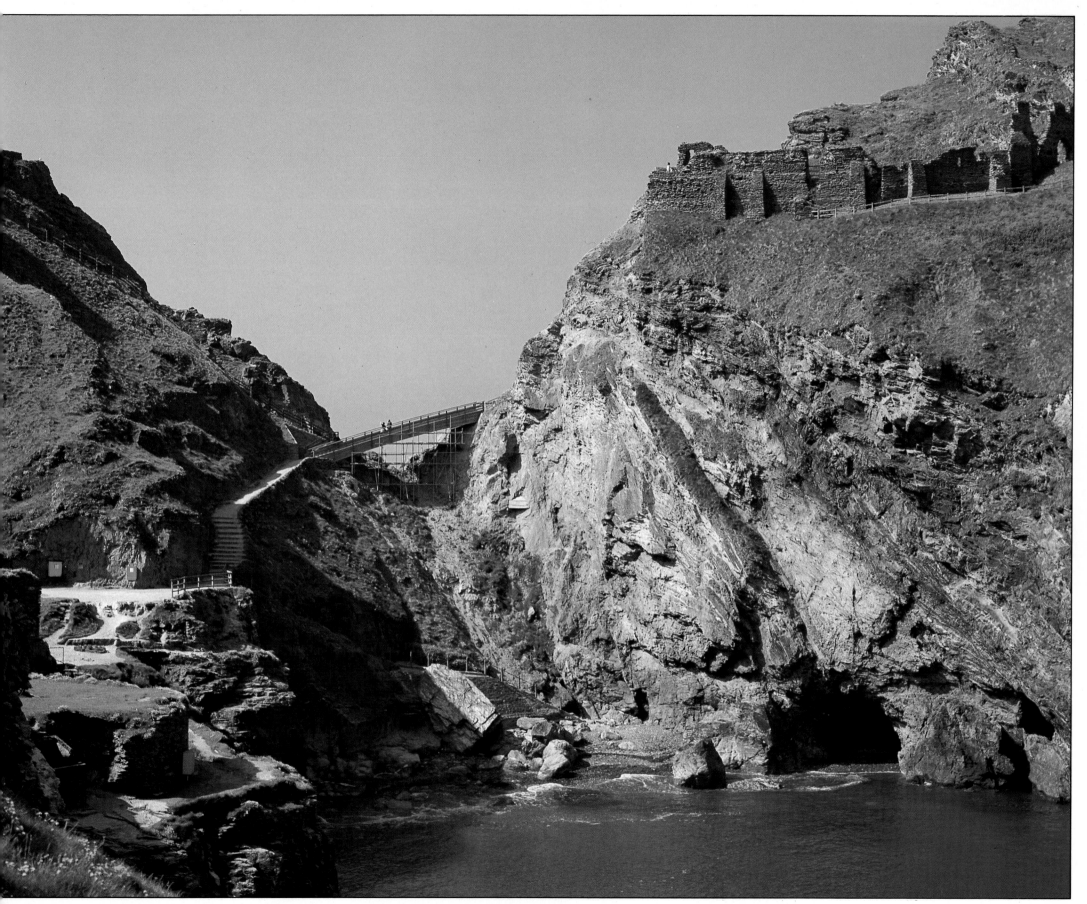

Cornwall. Facing page: boats stranded by low tide at Newquay. Above: the dramatic and romantic ruins of Tintagel Castle. Though the castle was built for Reginald, Earl of Cornwall, in 1145, it has long been associated with King Arthur and more recent research reveals that a monastery stood here in Arthurian times. Overleaf: (left) the fine sands and harbour of St Ives, whose old character remains largely unspoilt, and (right) Newquay Harbour.

Cornwall. Above: the Looe Estuary is lined by grassy fields and tree-covered hills, while boats lie stranded on the mudflats. Facing page: Whitesand Bay, which lies just to the north of Land's End. Overleaf: (left) the lonely hilltop church of St Endellion with its fine wagon-roof and (right) the charming town of St Ives, where a flourishing fishing industry regularly landed millions of pilchards in the course of a season.

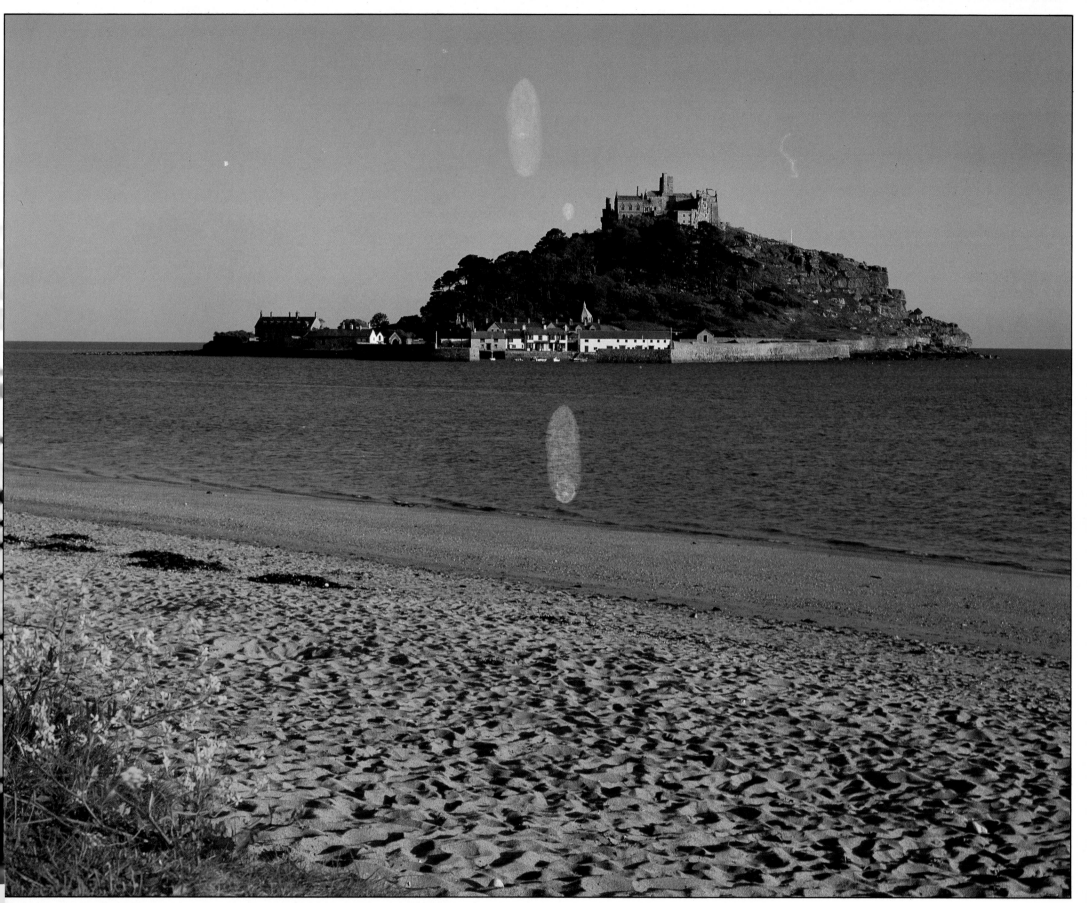

Cornwall. Facing page: Boscastle on the north coast whose narrow, winding entrance and towering cliffs provide almost perfect protection from the waves. Above: St Michael's Mount at high tide, when its causeway is covered by water. Overleaf: (left) Mullion Cove, whose cave can only be reached at low tide, and (right) Mevagissey.

35

Devon. Previous pages: (left) a heavily-laden donkey in Clovelly and (right) the River Exe flows past a pub at Bickleigh. Above: Kingswear on the Dart Estuary. Facing page: the 15th-century church at Combe Martin. Overleaf: the harbour at Brixham, where a statue of William of Orange records his first arrival on English soil, during the Glorious Revolution of 1688.

ERECTED BY PUBLIC SUBSCRIPTION
AND
DEDICATED TO THE TOWN OF BRIXHAM.
FOUNDATION STONE LAID 1ST NOV.Y 1888

BY HIS EXCELLENCY
COUNT DE BYLANDT.
UNVEILED 3RD NOVEMBER 1888. BY
C.A. BENTINCK ESQ. J.P.
THE RIGHT HON. LORD CHURSTON
CHAIRMAN OF COMMITTEE.

CHARLES.ARTHUR.J.SCARCHEN.

40

Devon. Above: the wild crags of the Valley of the Rocks, near Lynton. Facing page: the view from Orcombe Point.
Overleaf: (left) the choir and chancel and (right) the nave of Exeter Cathedral. The see came to Exeter in 1050, but the
present building only dates back to 1107, when the victorious Normans raised the Cathedral towers which we see today.

Devon. Facing page: Teignmouth, one of the oldest Devon resorts, has many fine buildings from last century. Above: the mile-long beach at Seaton, near the mouth of the River Yarty.

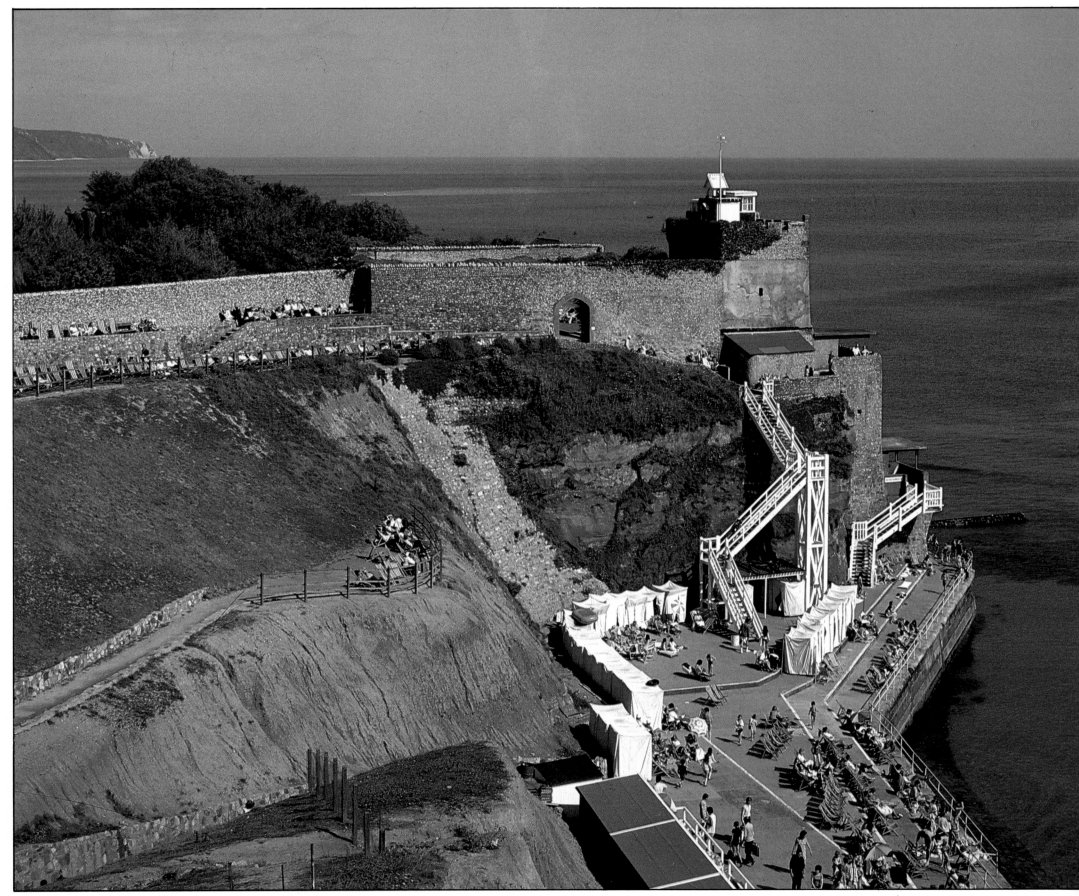

Devon. Above: Jacob's Ladder at Sidmouth, a pleasant seaside town packed with fine Regency buildings. Facing page: the harbour at Torquay, now the largest and grandest of the Devon resorts, with its fine beach and wide-ranging attractions and facilities.

Previous pages left and above: the Clifton Suspension Bridge, which was built in 1864 by Isambard Kingdom Brunel to link Somerset and Gloucestershire. Previous pages right: the Severn Bridge, constructed in 1966 with a central span of 3,200 feet, links the two sides of the Severn Estuary. Facing page: the magnificent cliffs of Cheddar Gorge, which rise to 450 feet and hide beautiful, stalactite-festooned caverns behind their faces.

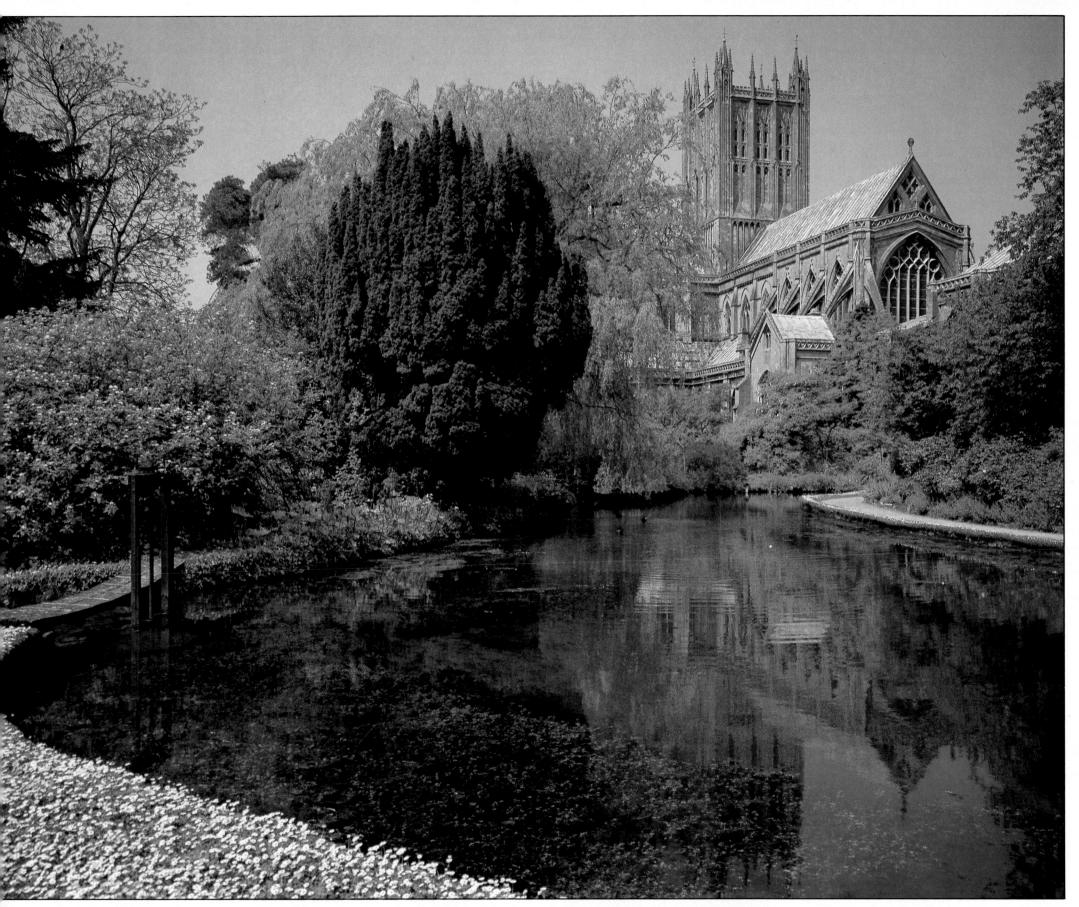

Above: the beautiful cathedral in the ecclesiastical city of Wells, Somerset, which was begun in 1180 and contains work from many subsequent periods. Wells' partner in the diocese is quite different, for Bath Abbey, Avon, (overleaf, shown left) with the Roman Baths in the foreground, is largely the product of a 16th century rebuilding. Facing page: the graceful sweep of Georgian town houses in The Circus in Bath, Avon, built by the Wood family, who were responsible for many of the city's fine buildings.

Avon. Previous pages: (left) a view of Bath from a hill to the east and (right) the East Front of Bath Abbey. Facing page: Bath Abbey's West Front, with its famous Jacob's Ladder carvings. Above and overleaf: the Florentine-style, shop-lined Pulteney Bridge, which crosses the Avon in the heart of Bath.

Dorset. Above: the charming thatched cottage at the end of a narrow lane in Higher Bockhampton where, in 1840, the novelist Thomas Hardy was born. Facing page: the lovely 15th-century Manor House at Athelhampton. Overleaf: (left) the natural arch of Durdle Door, carved out of the Purbeck limestone by the incessant waves, and (right) the peaceful seaside resort of Swanage.

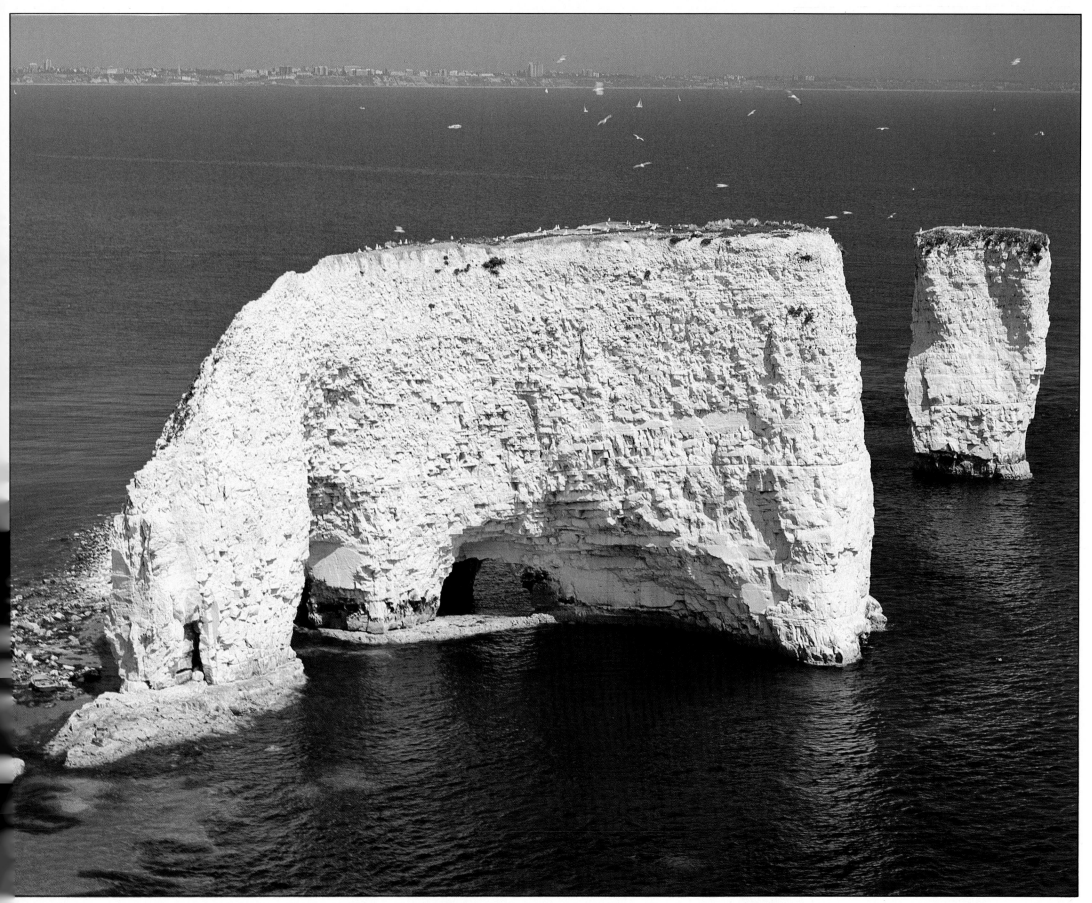

Dorset. Facing page and overleaf right: Durdle Door. Above: the dramatic chalk stacks of Old Harry Rocks. Overleaf left:
the beautiful sandy beach which lines Swanage Bay, in whose waters King Alfred the Great destroyed a fleet of Viking
ships in 877.

Above: the gaunt ruins of Corfe Castle dominate the skyline of Corfe, Dorset. Though the present buildings only date back to the 11th century, Corfe was a royal residence centuries earlier. In 978 King Edward the Martyr was murdered here by his stepmother and his body taken to Shaftesbury, (facing page) the street of Gold Hill, where he was buried in a convent founded by Alfred the Great.

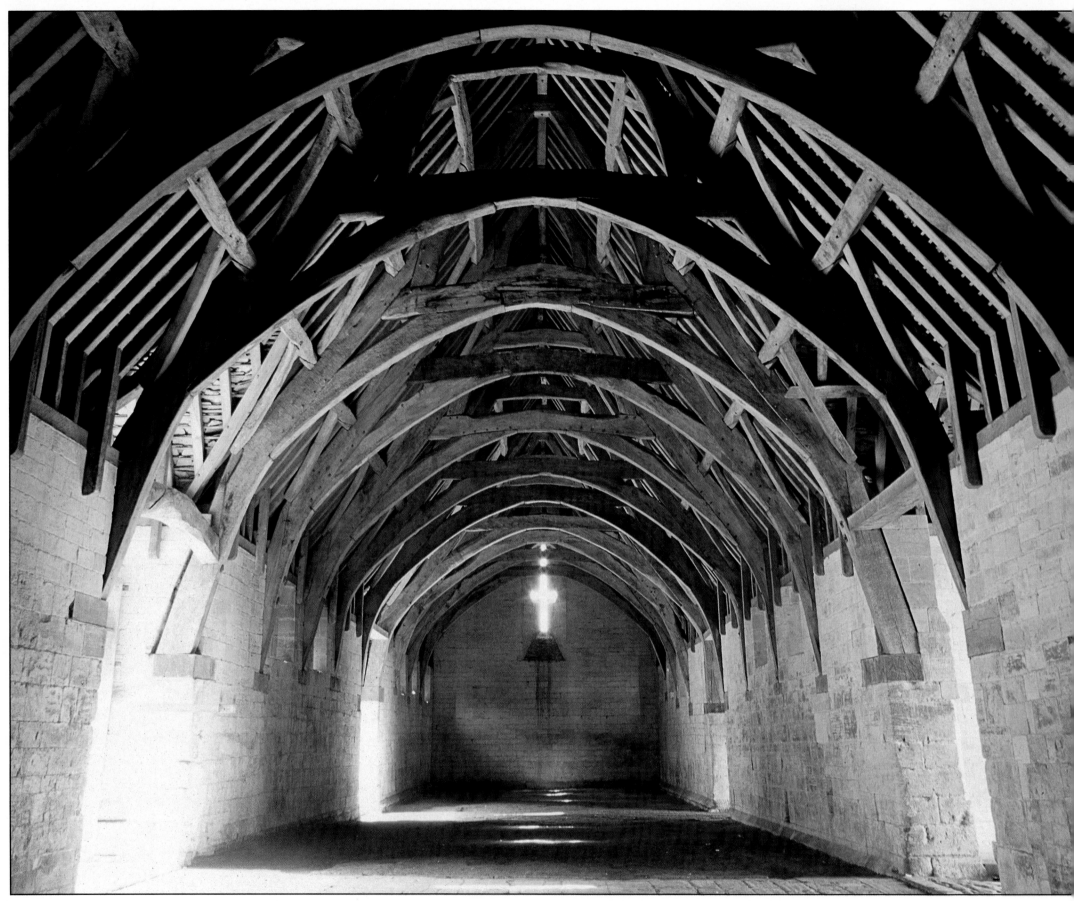
Wiltshire. Above: the 14th-century Tithe Barn in Bradford-on-Avon. Facing page: the tranquil church at Avebury, with its 15th century tower. Overleaf: (left) the magnificent cathedral at Salisbury, which was begun in 1220 and is a masterpiece of Early English Gothic architecture, and (right) the enigmatic outline of Stonehenge, which dates back thousands of years to a people long vanished from the land.

Wiltshire. Previous pages: (left) an aerial view of Salisbury Cathedral and (right) the altar at the Cathedral's east
nd. Facing page: the charming, stone village of Castle Combe, which once had a flourishing weaving industry. Above and
verleaf: the splendid Longleat House, home of the Marquess of Bath, was built in 1556 and boasts some magnificent state
oms, including the salon (overleaf left) and the drawing room (overleaf right).

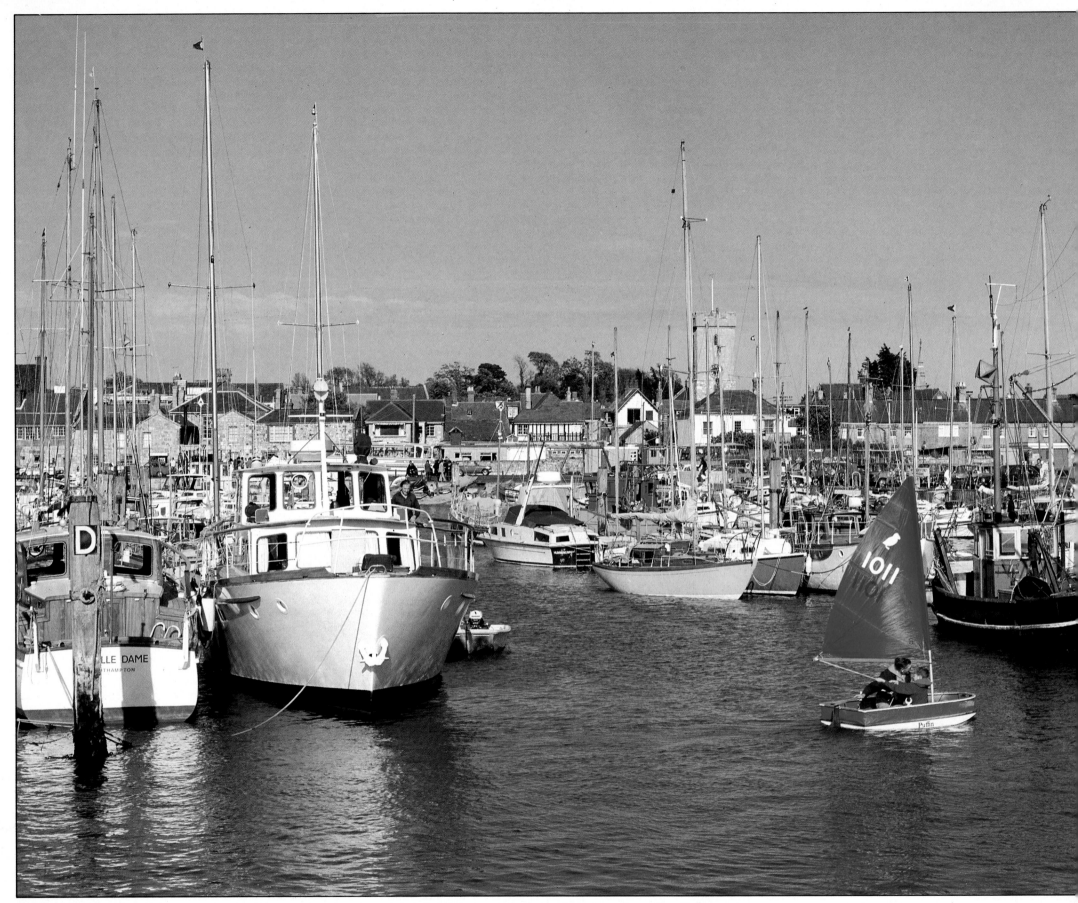

Above: Yarmouth, a small but delightful port on the Isle of Wight. Facing page: a yacht moored on the Stour at Christchurch, Hampshire, whose priory was begun in the 11th century by Flambard, one-time superintendent of the King's Kitchen. Overleaf: (left) a typical Dorset cottage and (right) a street scene in Lymington, a quiet resort town on the banks of the Boldre.

Above: pleasure boats moored at Lymington, Hampshire. Facing page: the excellent sands of Boscombe, Dorset. Overleaf: (left) an inn at East Grinstead, West Sussex, (right) flint cottages in West Dean, East Sussex.

Above: the mellow brick building of Glyndebourne, where a music and opera season was instituted in 1934 and has since become world famous. Facing page: the charming town of Midhurst in West Sussex. In 1834, the Duke of Devonshire inherited a small coastal village and set out to create from it a rival to the nearby town of Brighton. The result was Eastbourne (overleaf), a somewhat more genteel resort than its neighbour.

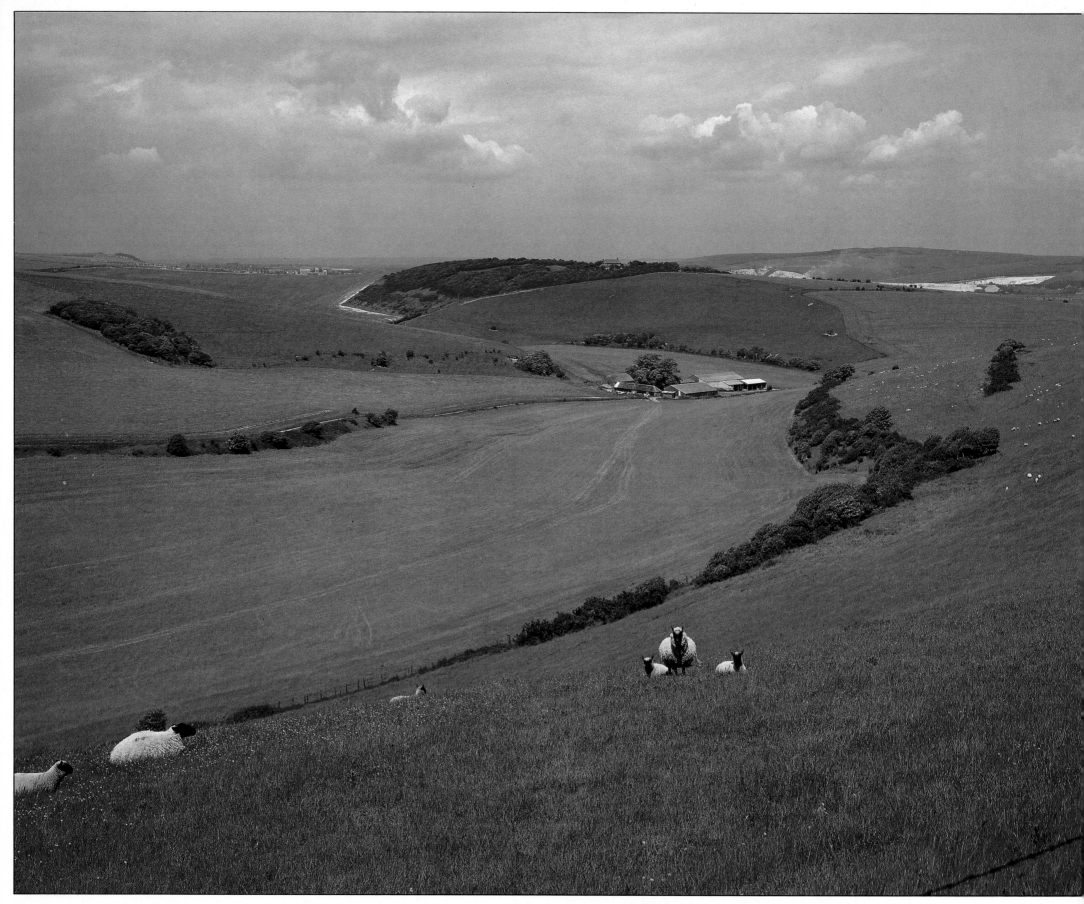

East Sussex. Above: the broad sweep of turf on the chalk downs near Lewes. Facing page: the long line of white cliffs which runs from Beachy Head to the Cuckmere River. Overleaf: (left) the beautifully-situated Bodiam Castle, which was built in 1385 as protection against an invasion from France, and (right) the bizarrely-extravagant Royal Pavilion at Brighton, built for the Prince Regent early last century.

East Sussex. Above: Eastbourne. Facing page: the lighthouse and cliffs at Beachy Head, the towering chalk face which rises more than 500 feet above the sea, creating the highest cliffs on the south coast. Overleaf: (left) a hunt readies for the off and (right) the rooftops of the bustling old town of Rye, a member of the Cinque Ports.

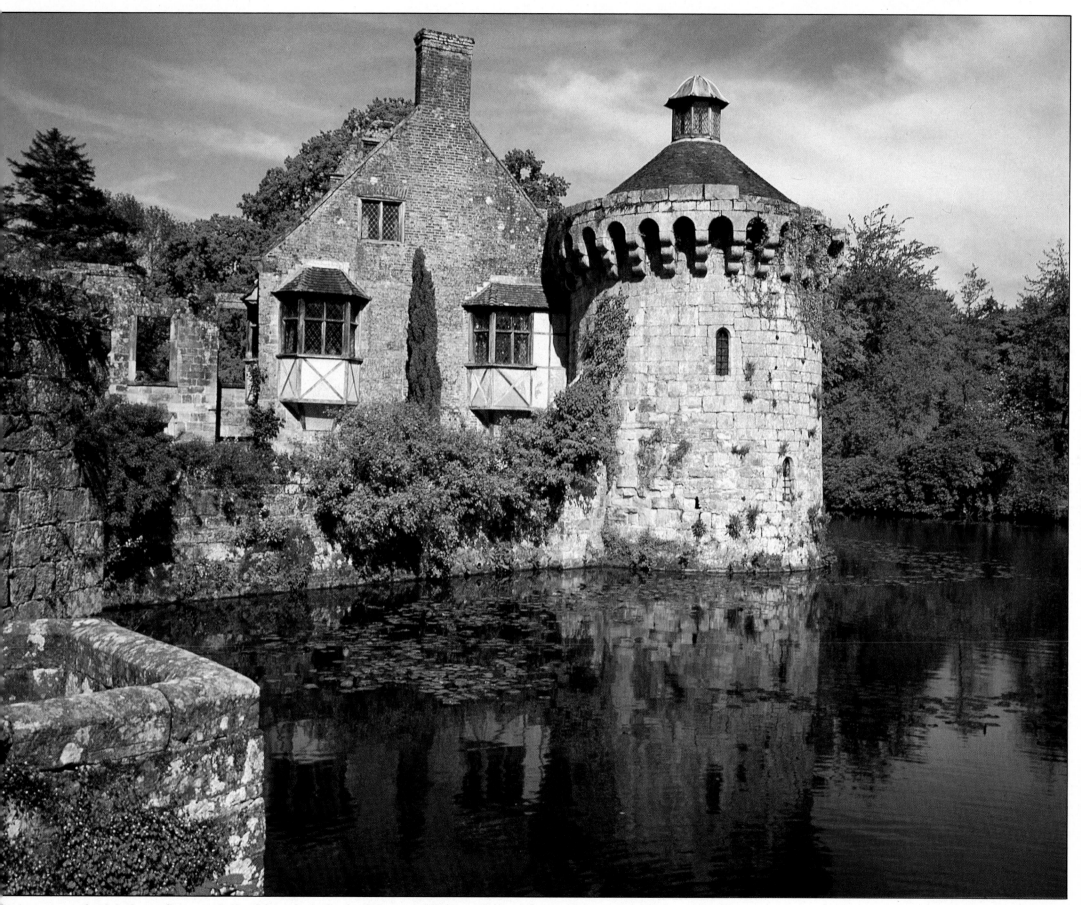

Facing page: the Medway flows quietly through Aylesford, a pretty Kent village. Above: the picturesque remnants of Kent's Scotney Castle, built in 1378, which stand in the grounds of a 19th-century mansion. Overleaf: (left) the gracious Pantiles in Royal Tunbridge Wells, the most fashionable area of the town in its heyday as a spa during the 18th century, and (right) the Mermaid, which dates back to 1420, in Rye, East Sussex.

Kent. Facing page: the massive, early 14th-century gatehouse of Tonbridge Castle, perhaps the town's finest landmark.
Above: Hever Castle, the girlhood home of Anne Boleyn. Overleaf: (left) the Georgian Guildhall and the Market Place in
Faversham and (right) West Gate gardens in Canterbury.

Kent. Above: the Pantiles at Royal Tunbridge Wells. Facing page: the weatherboarded mill at Farningham. Overleaf: (left) the harbour at Ramsgate, a resort which can boast some fine Victorian buildings, and (right) the magnificent mediaeval structure of Canterbury Cathedral, mother church of the Church of England, which stands on the site where St Augustine first brought the Gospel to England in 597.

Kent. Above: Knole House, one of the finest stately homes in England, which has a room for each day of the year and a staircase for each week. Facing page: colourful gardens and timbered houses in Headcorn. Overleaf: (left) the fine collection of Tudor houses known as the Weavers, in Canterbury, and (right) some of the Tudor and Jocobean buildings which are such a feature of Chilham.

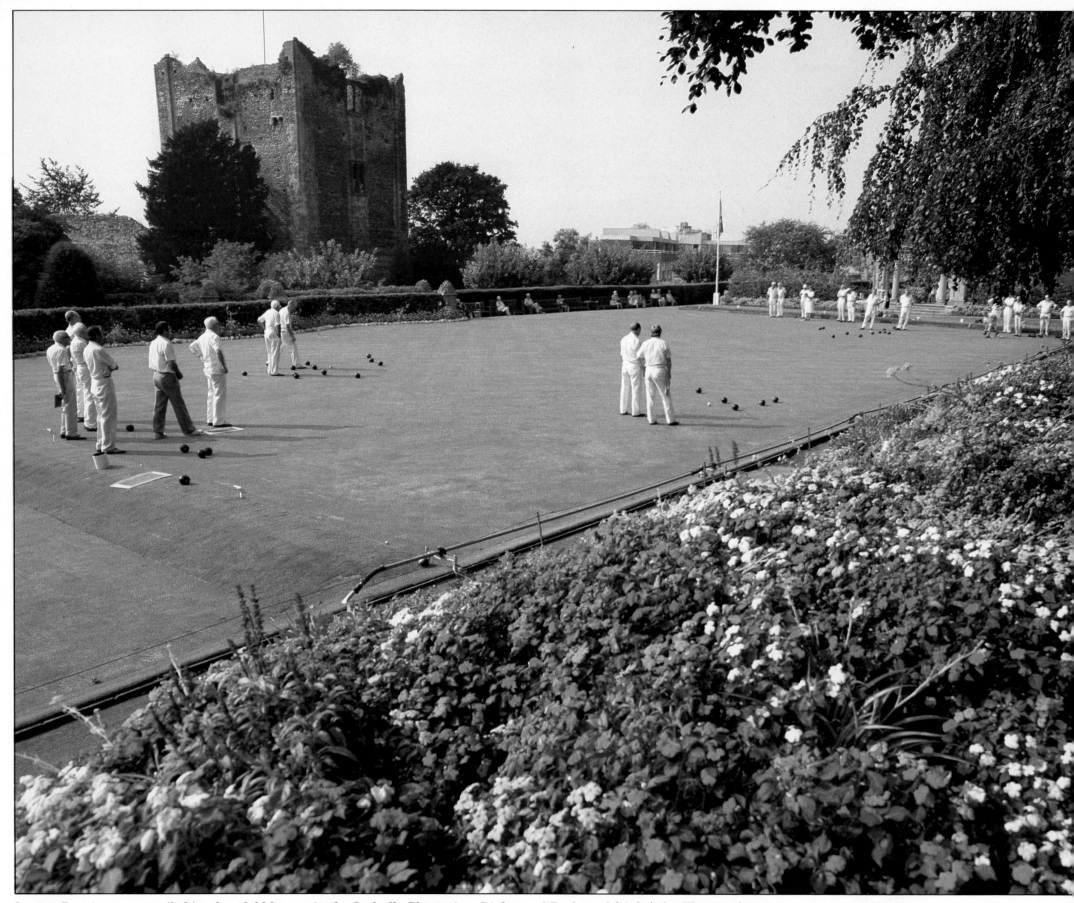

Surrey. Previous pages: (left) colourful blooms in the Isabella Plantation, Richmond Park, and (right) the Thames from Richmond Hill. Above and overleaf right: the massive Norman keep which is nearly all that remains of Guildford Castle. Facing page: Guildford High Street. Overleaf left: the modern brick edifice of Guildford Cathedral, which was completed in 1961 in a simplified Gothic style to the designs of Sir Edward Maufe.

Surrey. Above: the Tudor, red-brick mansion of Sutton Place, near Guildford. Facing page: rhododendrons in bloom at Oakwood Hill Church. Overleaf: (left) cottages near Outwood, the center of a 2,000 acre National Trust area, and (right) in Claygate.

Surrey. Above: a broad field of growing maize near Shere. Facing page: well turned out horses at a ploughing competition at Godalming.

Surrey. Previous pages: (left) a landscape near Guildford and (right) Broadwater Lake, Godalming. Above: part of the herd of deer in Richmond Park. Facing page: the Chinese Pagoda in Kew Gardens, reputedly the most famous botanical gardens in the world. Overleaf: Hampton Court Palace, (left) the classical Wren facade added by William and Mary at the end of the 17th century and (right) part of the orignal 16th century palace erected for Cardinal Wolsey, together with an elaborate clock installed by King Henry VIII.

Surrey. Above: Epsom Racecourse on Derby Day, the country's premier event for three-year-olds and a major occasion in the sporting calendar. Facing page: racehorses exercising nearby. Overleaf: two creeper-festooned homes, (left) a cottage near Lingfield and (right) Winkworth Farmhouse, near the famous arboretum at Hascombe.

Surrey. Previous pages: (left) the Centre Court of the All England Lawn Tennis and Croquet Club at Wimbledon, which has witnessed many memorable tennis matches, and (right) Kew Gardens. Facing page: the Priest's House at Leigh. Above: the village clock in Abinger Hammer which, as its name suggests, was a center of the Surrey iron-working industry in the h century.

London. Above: the Royal Festival Hall on the South Bank which hosts a wide range of events and can hold an audience of over 3,000. Facing page: Oxford Street at night. Overleaf: (left) the beautiful interior of Wren's St Mary-at-Hill, with woodwork by William Gibbs Rogers, and (right) the interior of St Martin's-in-the-Field, which contains both a Royal and an Admiralty Box.

London. Above: the familiar east front of Buckingham Palace, which contains 600 rooms and is the London residence of the sovereign. Facing page: the Palace of Westminster, though still referred to as a palace, is the seat of government and bears little resemblance to the mediaeval palace which it replaced after a disastrous fire in 1834. Overleaf: (left) the Chapel of St Stephen's in the Palace of Westminster, and (right) the 13th-century Westminster Abbey.

CHRISTUS FACTUS EST PRO NOBIS OBEDIENS USQUE AD MORTEM CRUCIS

London. Facing page: Piccadilly Circus. Above: the setting sun silhouettes the Palace of Westminster, which is largely a 19th-century building containing both Houses of Parliament and innumerable offices. Overleaf: (left) a coach and four exercising in Hyde Park, and (right) the fish counter in Harrods, London's most famed department store.

TODAYS MARKET of SMOKED FISH

Smoked Haddock	1·80
" Fillet	1·90
" Cod Fillet	1·90
" Cod Roe	3·80
" Trout	1·20 EACH
" Eel FILLET	7·50
" WHOLE	3·80
" Mackerel	1·40
" Salmon	12·00
Smokies	1·45
Golden Cutlets	N/A
Buckling/Bloater	1·40
Kippers Loch Fyne	1·20
" Filleted	1·30
" Manx	1·40
Smoked Sprat Fillet	3·50
GRAV-LAX	WHOLE 2·50 / 11·00

TODAYS MARKET of SHELL FISH

Oysters	60p
Crevettes	7·00
Crab Claws	8·50
Lobster Tails	9·00
Cockles	1·75
Winkles	
Escallops	4·00
Mussels	1·75
Lobsters	8·00
Crab	2·00
Crab Meat white/brown	7·00
Dublin Bay Prawns	4·00
Tails	
Crawfish	5·50
Prawns Eng.	
Prawns Norway	
Shrimps	
King Prawns	

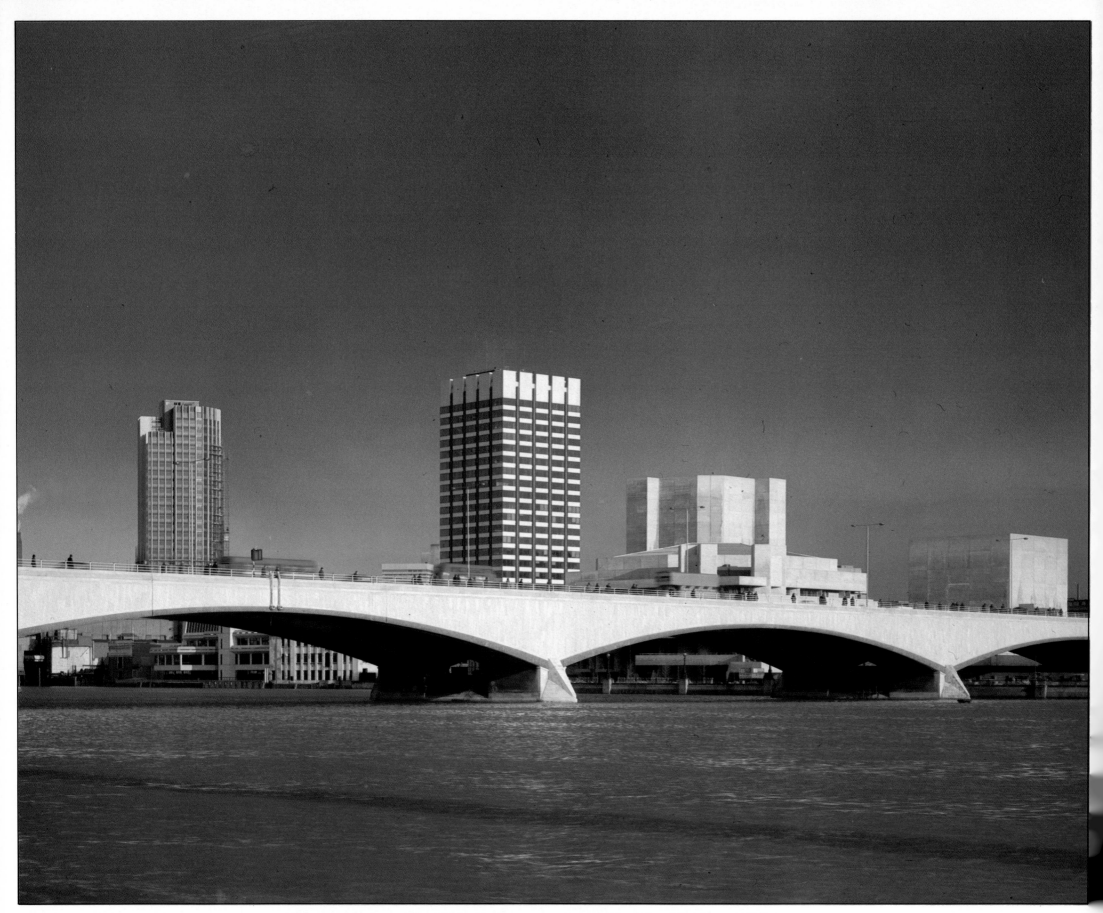

London. Above: the reinforced concrete Waterloo Bridge of the 1930s. Facing page: the ornate Albert Bridge of 1873, which has recently been strengthened. Overleaf: (left) the Armourers' and Brasiers' Hall, rebuilt in 1840, and (right) the Egyptian Hall at Mansion House as laid for lunch for the incoming and outgoing Lord Mayor after the annual election on Michaelmas Day.

London. Above: the St Stephen's Tower of the Palace of Westminster, which contains the famous 13-ton bell known as Big Ben. Facing page: the City at sunset. Overleaf: (left) the Apothecaries' Hall, which was built in 1668 after the original had been destroyed in the Great Fire, and (right) the Princes' Chamber in the Palace of Westminster, which serves as the ante-room to the House of Lords.

These pages: two opposing views across the Thames. Above: the Palace of Westminster from County Hall. Facing page: the Edwardian Renaissance edifice of County Hall from the Palace of Westminster. Overleaf: Windsor, Berkshire; (left) Church Street and (right) the mighty castle, which stands on a hill overlooking the Thames and has guarded the western approaches to London since the days of William the Conqueror.

Berkshire. Although Windsor Castle dates back more than nine centuries, its interior has been restyled many times and is the work of generations of architects and designers. Above: St George's Hall, with the royal thrones and the arms of the Knights of the Garter. Overleaf: (left) the King's Dining Room and (right) the Grand Reception Room, decorated in the style of Louis XV. (Pictures Crown Copyright Reserved).

174

…erkshire. Windsor Castle is still used by the Royal Family and contains many splendid State Apartments. Facing page: …he thrones and their elaborate canopy in St George's Hall. Above: the Queen's Drawing Room. Overleaf: the Queen's …resence Chamber. (Pictures Crown Copyright Reserved).

erkshire. Previous pages: (left) the King's State Bed Chamber and (right) the magnificent Waterloo Chamber, both in indsor Castle. (Pictures Crown Copyright Reserved). Facing page: Church Street, Windsor. Above: the imposing entrance the South Front of Windsor Castle from Home Park.

Previous pages: (left) the Hambledon Mill, which stands on a site where a mill has stood since 1338, and (right) Prior's Croft, one of several picturesque cottages in Dorney, both in Buckinghamshire. Facing page: the partly-Norman church at Medmenham, Buckinghamshire. Above: Ye Olde Bell, close to the ruined monastery where a sister of King Edward the Confessor lies buried, in Hurley, Berkshire.

185

Oxfordshire. Above: the charming little village of Whitchurch. Facing page: the lock at Goring, which is busy with holiday boats during the summer. Overleaf: Henley and the crowds that attend its famous regatta. Instituted in 1829, the regatta rapidly became a noted social venue and remains so to this day, with some of the visitors paying more attention to society than boat racing.

Oxfordshire. Facing page: the majestic Blenheim Palace at Woodstock, which was presented to the Duke of Marlborough in 1722 in recognition of his victories in battle against the French. Above: the squat tower of Merton College, one of the oldest colleges in Oxford, having been founded in 1264 by Walter de Merton, Bishop of Rochester.

Oxfordshire. Oxford University is one of the oldest seats of learning in Europe and its colleges can boast some of the finest buildings in the country. Previous pages: (left) Wren's Sheldonian Theatre of 1664, now used for functions, and (right) Nuffield College, founded in 1937 for postgraduates. Facing page: the soaring tower of Magdalen College and traditional punts on the Isis. Above: Christ Church, founded by Cardinal Wolsey in 1525. Overleaf: (left) the Bridge of Sighs, part of Hertford College and (right) University College, the oldest college.

195

Oxfordshire. The buildings associated with the university in Oxford have sometimes changed their uses. The Radcliffe Camera (previous pages left) of 1737 was orginally a camera obscura, but now serves as a reading room. Others, such as (previous pages right and facing page) Oriel College and (above) St John's College, remain as accomodation for undergraduates.

Gloucestershire. Above: the neatly-kept village of Moreton-in-Marsh. Facing page: Bourton-on-the-Water. Overleaf left: Gloucester Cathedral, which was begun as an abbey church in 1089 and contains exceptionally fine work from almost every period of mediaeval architecture, and (overleaf right) the squat tower of Tewkesbury Abbey dominates the town.

Gloucestershire. Above: the almost archetypal Cotswold village of Bibury stands on the River Coln. Facing page: the mill at Lower Slaughter. Overleaf: (left) the solid mass of Tewkesbury Abbey, which stands as it did on May 4, 1471, when one of the bloodiest battles of the Wars of the Roses raged around the town, and (right) Chipping Campden seen through the arches of its Jacobean market hall.

ucestershire. Facing page: the beautiful gardens and subdued architecture of the manor at Hidcote. Above: the mellow
one cottages of Naunton.

Hereford and Worcester. Above: the charming town of Ross-on-Wye stands on a hill overlooking a curve in the river, and benefited from a remarkably early effort at town planning by John Kyrle around 1700. Facing page: the quaint Church Lane in the small market town of Ledbury. Overleaf: two very different, but equally charming cottages in the county.

212

Hereford and Worcester. These pages: charming, picturesque Broadway is one of the most visited villages, yet it has not become commercialised, apart from a profusion of antique shops and retains much of its original atmosphere. Overleaf: (left) Worcester Cathedral and (right) the interesting group of ecclesiastical buildings at the heart of Evesham, made up of the 12th-century All Saints', the 16th-century St Lawrence's and the Perpendicular bell tower of the abbey which once stood here.

Previous pages: the cathedral at Worcester, which was begun in 1084 by Bishop St Wulfstan, one of the few English prelates to keep his position after the Norman Conquest. Work continued for generations and the Early English style was used to build the soaring nave and chancel. Facing page: a typical thatched, timbered cottage of the county. Above: the remnant of the once-vast Pershore Abbey, together with the smaller St Andrew's Church.

Above: Packwood House, Warwickshire, is a lovely example of a Tudor building. Facing page: Compton Wynyates, one of the most charming Tudor mansions in Warwickshire. Overleaf: (left) central Birmingham, the second largest city in the nation, and (right) central Coventry with the new Cathedral and the ruins of the old, destroyed along with much of the city by German bombers on November 14th, 1940.

Warwickshire. Stratford-upon-Avon is rich in associations with William Shakespeare. His bones lie in Holy Trinity Church (above) while his plays are performed at the Royal Shakespeare Theatre (facing page) built in 1932. Nearby, at Shottery, can be found Anne Hathaway's Cottage (overleaf right), where Shakespeare courted his future wife. Overleaf left: Welford-on-Avon, which lies four miles to the southwest.

Above: the 82-arch Harringworth and Welland Railway Viaduct of 1879, Northamptonshire. Facing page: the 17th-century Houghton Mill, Cambridgeshire, which is believed to be the oldest on the River Ouse.

Cambridgeshire. The first college at Cambridge University was founded in 1284, although scholars had been present here for nearly a century and it was not until 1571 that the university was formally incorporated. The greatest treasures of the university are its buildings: (above) Christ's College, founded in 1439; (facing page) the Senate House; (overleaf left) St John's College, founded by the mother of Henry VII and (overleaf right) King's College Chapel.

...bridgeshire. The architecture of the college buildings reveals much about their history: (facing page) the impressive
...or gateway to St John's College; (above) the elegant 17th-century buildings of Clare College; (overleaf left) the
...nificent King's College Chapel, considered by many to be the finest Gothic building in Europe, with its fine
...ework and exquisite stained glass, and (overleaf right) Trinity College's Great Gate of 1519.

Above: snow covers the ground around the 14th-century church at Earls Colne, Essex. Facing page: the green and pond at Finchingfield, Essex, one of the prettiest views in the county. Overleaf: (left) the watersplash in Kersey, one of the most picturesque villages in Suffolk and formerly famous for its cloth, and (right) the pastel shades of the cottages in Cavendish, Suffolk.

Facing page: Hurstbourne Tarrant. Above: brightly-coloured poppies border a Suffolk field. Overleaf: some of the charmingly-uneven buildings in Lavenham, Suffolk, once a prosperous wool town where the author of the nursery rhyme *Twinkle, twinkle little star* lived.

248

Above: the Jocobean mansion that is Blickling Hall, Norfolk. The house was built in the early 17th century for Sir Henry Hobart and, though it has undergone many additions and alterations, its basic Jacobean character remains unchanged.
Facing page: boats at Potter Heigham, a popular centre for the Norfolk Broads. Overleaf: the cobbled Steep Hill in Lincoln, which leads up to the splendid mediaeval cathedral.

Derbyshire. Above: Chatsworth House, the home of the Duke of Devonshire and one of the great homes of England. Built for the 1st Duke around 1700, Chatsworth is a masterpiece of elegance and stands in vast acres of parkland which include the tallest fountain in Britain. Facing page: the Derwent at Matlock Bath, one of the most popular spas of the last century.

Yorkshire. The bleak splendour of the North Yorkshire Moors (these pages) has a beauty which appeals to the wilder instincts, though some find them too barren for comfort. Overleaf: (left) a typical view of Bradford, with Victorian Gothic standing beside modern concrete structures, and (right) the picturesque Shambles in the heart of York.

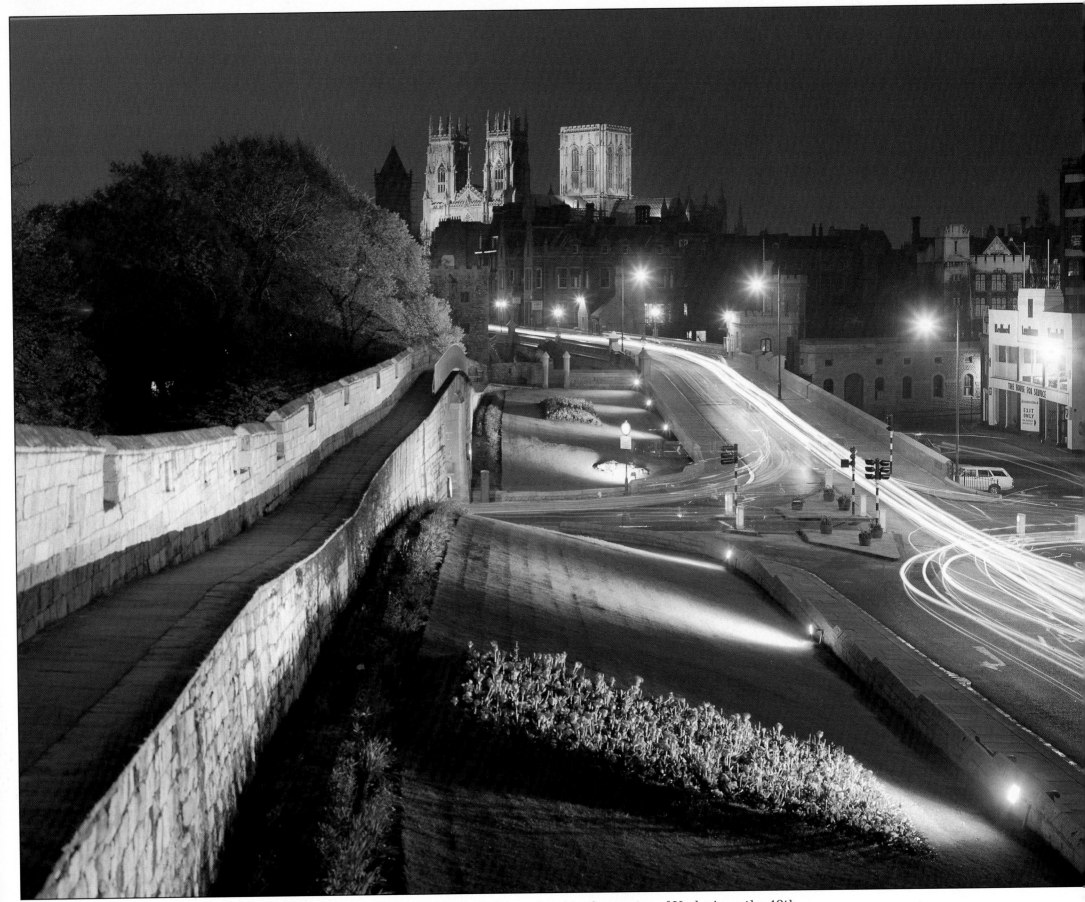

Yorkshire. The magnificent York Minster (previous pages and these pages) has stood in the centre of York since the 13th century and is one of the most beautiful churches in England. The recent fire which caused so much damage to the Minster only added to the burden of restoration work which has been underway in recent years. Overleaf: (left) Bainbridge in Wensleydale, the valley which gave its name to a particularly tasty cheese, and (right) Bransdale.

It was at the fishing port of Whitby (previous pages), Yorkshire, that the church synod was held in 664 which committed England to the Roman rather than the Celtic rite. Above: the vast Humber Bridge, Humberside, which crosses the river west of Kingston-upon-Hull and is the longest bridge in the country. Facing page: Rievaulx Abbey, Yorkshire, which was founded in 1131 and once housed a community of 600 holy men, though only 22 remained by the time of its dissolution.

Previous pages: the fine, timber-framed houses of central Chester, Cheshire, some of which date back to mediaeval times, though many are Victorian constructions. Liverpool: (above) the spectacularly-modern interior of the circular Roman Catholic Cathedral; (facing page) the legendary Liver Birds perched atop the Royal Liver Building; (overleaf left) the Grapes and (overleaf right) the Philharmonic, two of the city's pubs.

Previous pages: Liverpool. These pages: the seaside resort of Blackpool, whose sands stretch for seven miles, and its most famous landmark, the 520-foot-tall Tower of 1895. Overleaf left: Blackpool Tower's famous ballroom. Overleaf right: the 15th-century parish church which became Manchester Cathedral when that diocese was created in 1847.

Cumbria. Above: rushes stand along the margins of Derwent Water, the widest lake in the Lake District. Facing page: bare winter trees beside Ullswater. Overleaf: (left) the natural Small Water, high above the artificial lake of Haweswater Reservoir, and (right) Grasmere, where Wordsworth wrote some of his best-known works.

282

imbria. Facing page: Ullswater. Above: a tumbling beck in Scandale. Overleaf: (left) the cold light of dawn creeps rough the mist and casts long shadows across the banks of Ullswater, and (right) Derwent Water from Lady's Rake.

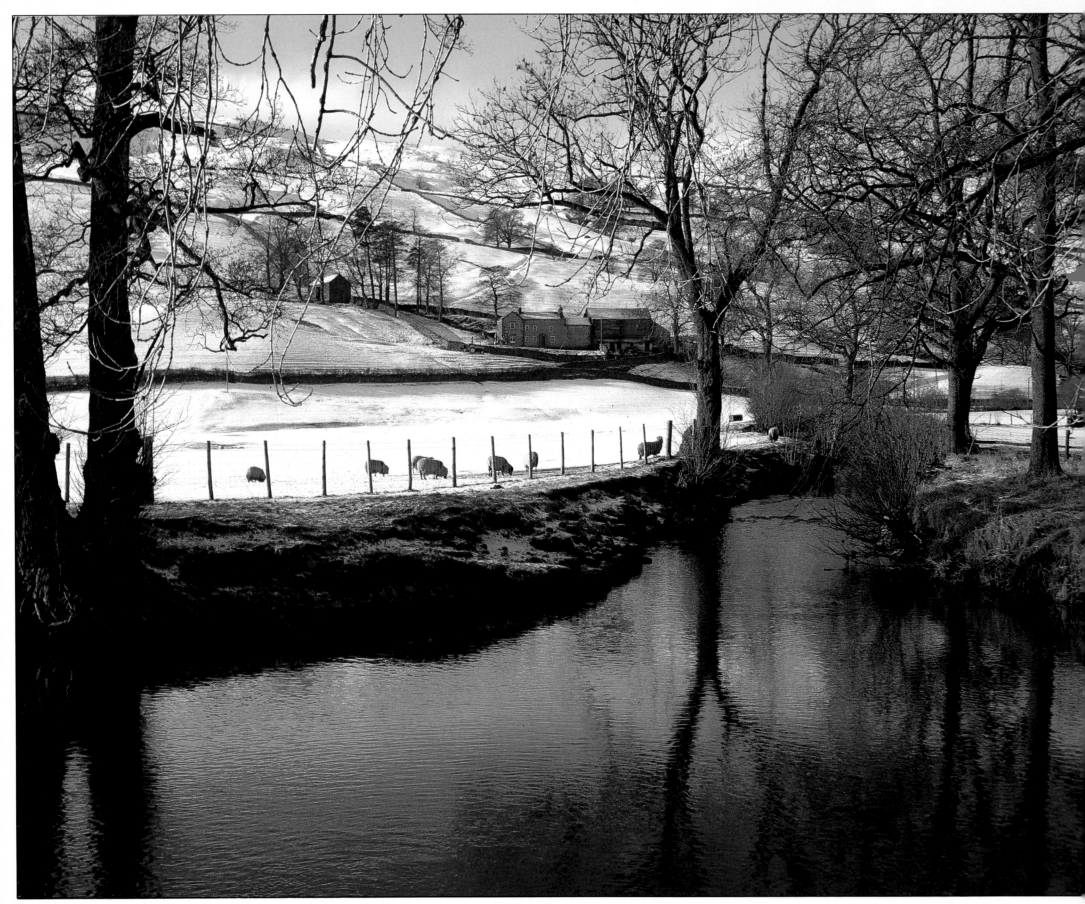

Cumbria. Above: the River Sprint beside Tom's Howe Farm in Longsleddale. Facing page: the Kirkstile Inn and its accompanying church nestled beneath the towering crags which make this one of the most spectacularly-sited pubs in the kingdom. Overleaf: (left) the silky, rushing waters of High Force, a waterfall in Gowbarrow Park, above Ullswater, and (right) row boats for hire at Bowness-on-Windermere.

Cumbria. Above: the grey waters of Blea Tarn lie ruffled by an autumn wind. Facing page: a view of Haweswater, in reality a reservoir, from the east shore looking towards Kidsty Pike and the long ridge known as High Street. It was along this 2,500-foot-high ridge that the Romans built a military road from Windermere to near Penrith.

Previous pages: views of Whitby Harbour, (left) from the steps leading up to Whitby Abbey and (right) from the harbour itself. Facing page: the iron Tyne Bridge and brightly painted Swing Bridge in Newcastle-upon-Tyne. Above: the floodlit towers of Durham Cathedral rise above River Wear as they have done for nearly nine centuries.

Previous pages: (left) climbers in Craig Ddu, Powys, and (right) a quiet lane in the Gwydwr Forest, near Betws-y-Coed, Gwynedd. Above: the Cader Idris Mountains in winter. Facing page: the Dee River rushes over shallows near Llangollen. Overleaf: (left) the high-sided ravine of Fairy Glen, Gwynedd, and (right) Craig Ddu in Powys.

Previous pages: (left) a low sun shines weakly through the mist in the Ogwen Valley, Gwynedd, and (right) Cardiff City Hall. Above: a sheep pauses in its grazing as a helicopter swoops low over Gwynedd's Cader Range. Facing page: the massive, Norman defences of Dyfed's Pembroke Castle, with its 75-foot-tall keep. Overleaf: (left) Lake Ogwen, Gwynedd, (right) a winter view of Caerphilly Castle, Mid Glamorgan, the largest in Wales.

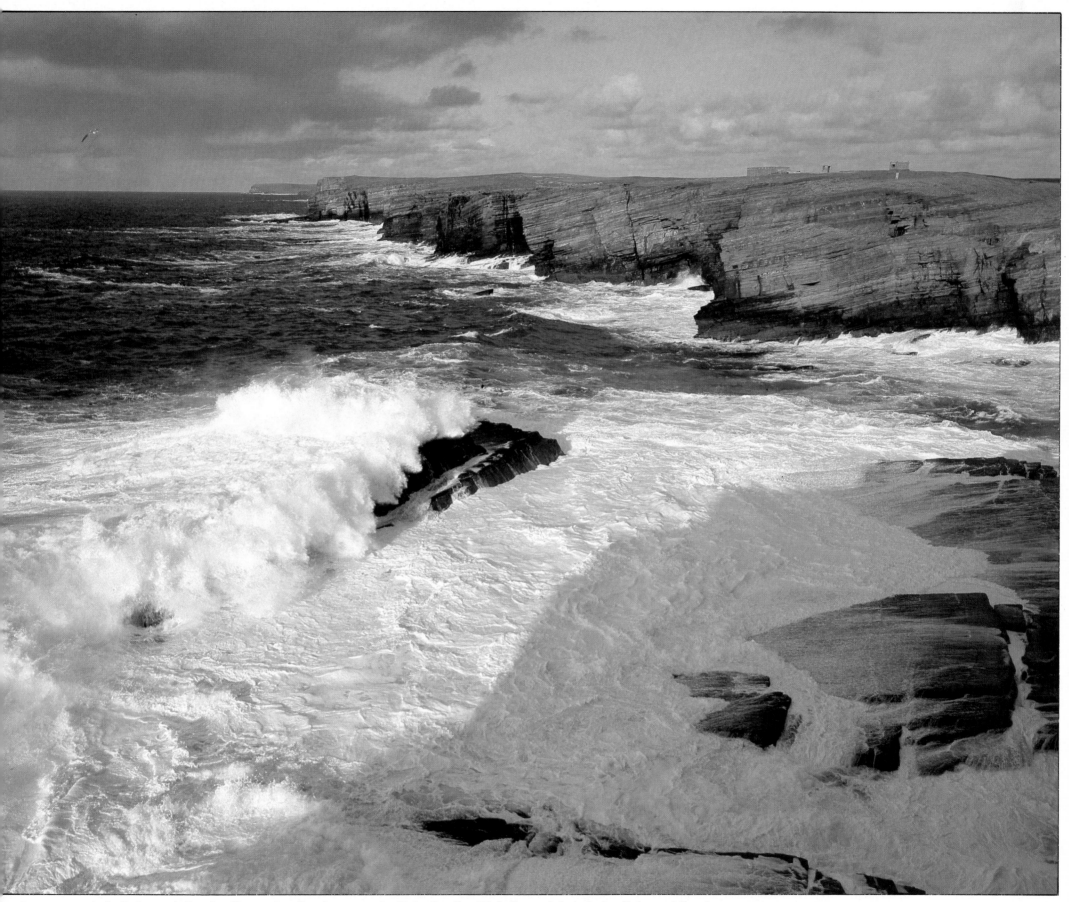

Previous pages left: Balmoral Castle, Grampian Region, as rebuilt in the Scottish Baronial style by Prince Albert, Consort of Queen Victoria, in 1852. Previous pages right: the snows of Glencoe, Highland Region. Facing page: a view of the River Tay from Kinnoull Hill near Perth, Tayside. Above: a view north along the Noust of Bigging Bay on Mainland, in the Orkney Islands. Overleaf: (left) the River Beathach in Glen Orchy, and (right) Eilean Donnan Castle, Highland Region.

cing page: the Caledonian Canal at Corpach, Highland Region. Above: a yacht on the still waters of Loch Creran at
nset. Overleaf: (left) the modern Inverlochy Castle, Highland Region, which replaced the structure near which the
arquis of Montrose gained one of his greatest victories in 1645, and (right) Kilchurn Castle, Strathclyde, long the
ome of the Breadalbane family, was garrisoned by Hanoverian troops during the rising of Bonnie Prince Charlie in 1745.

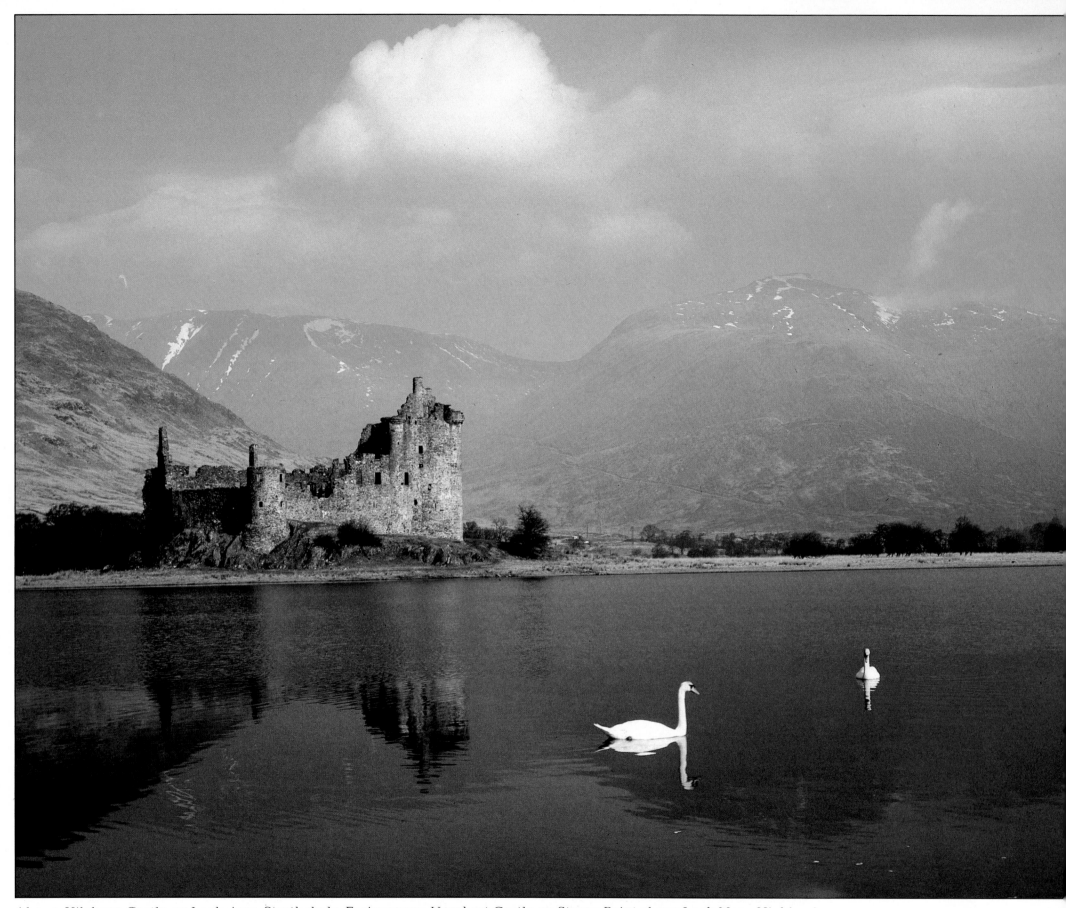

Above: Kilchurn Castle on Loch Awe, Strathclyde. Facing page: Urquhart Castle on Strone Point above Loch Ness, Highland Region. Overleaf: (left) Loch Tummel, Tayside Region, which has recently been dammed and extended, and (right) Inverary Castle, Strathclyde, seat for five centuries of the Duke of Argyll, head of the clan Campbell, who is known to his clansmen as the MacCailean Mor, son of the great Colin.

These pages: the two great bridges which cross the Firth of Forth. Above: the cantilevered rail bridge which was built between 1883 and 1890 and whose two main spans each cover 1,710 feet. Right: the modern suspension road bridge whose central span stretches over 3,300 feet. Overleaf: (left) a crisp autumn day at Loch Moy, Highland Region, and (right) the frozen waters of Loch Morlich, Highland Region, in winter.

These pages: Edinburgh Castle, whose natural defences have been so improved by man that it is only known to have fallen twice in all its long and turbulent history: once in 1296, when Edward I of England captured it, and again in 1341, when the Scots took it back. Overleaf: (left) Balmoral Castle, Grampian Region, in winter and (right) Kilchurn Castle, Strathclyde Region, whose keep was built as a refuge for Sir Colin Campbell and his family in 1440.

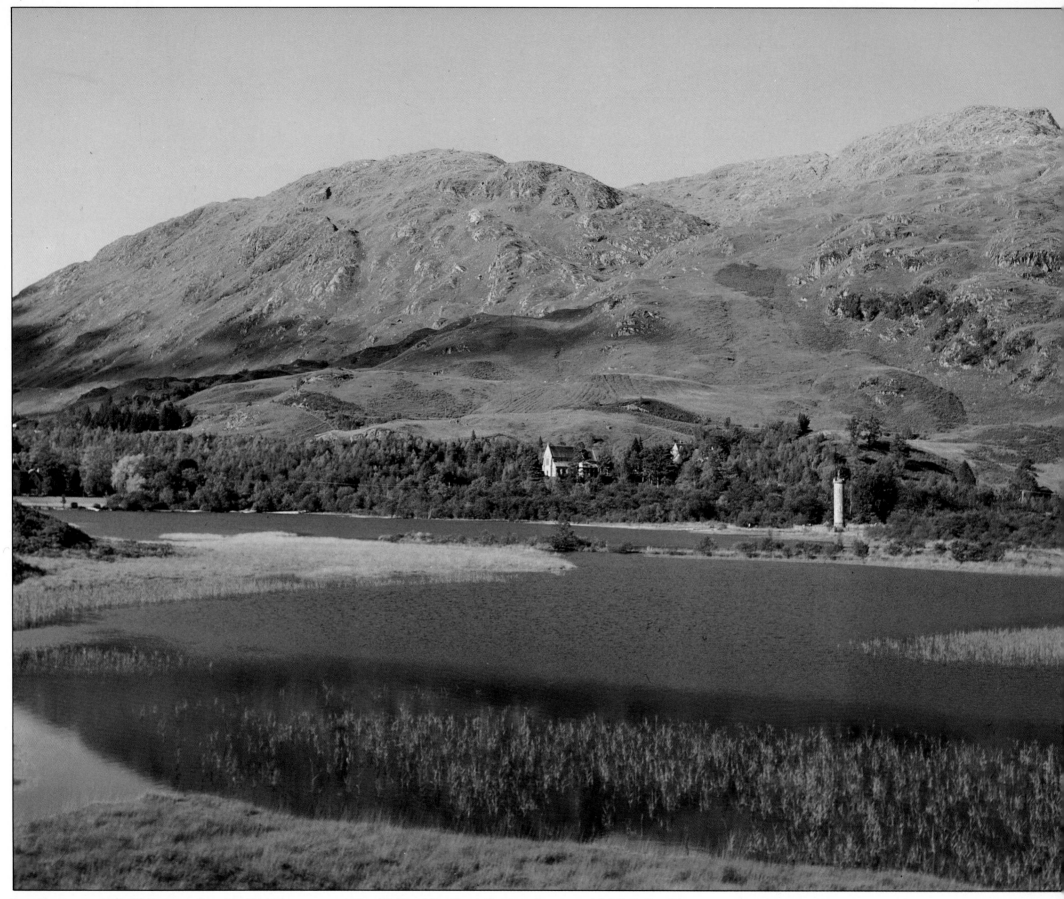

Previous pages: (left) the road and rail bridges across the Firth of Forth at Queensferry, and (right) the River
Dochart, Central Region. Above: Glenfinnan, Highland Region, where Bonnie Prince Charlie raised his standard on August
19th, 1745, before marching south with his loyal clans, reaching Derby before being forced to retreat to eventual defeat
at Culloden. Facing page: the world-famous Gleneagles Hotel, Tayside Region, and its golf links.

ious pages: (left) the ruins of Castle Moil beside the harbour of Kyleakin, Isle of Skye, and (right) Loch Linnhe,
hland Region. Facing page: the Glenfinnan Viaduct, Highland Region. Above: the small fishing village of Plockton, on
h Carron, Highland Region.

Above: the lighthouse at Torneady Point on the Aran Islands. Facing page: Gosford Castle, built as a large, Norman-style mansion in the early 19th-century by Thomas Hopper, stands at Markethill in Co. Armagh. Overleaf: scenes of Irish life.

St Patrick's Purgatory (above) on Station Island in the inland lake of Lough Derg, Co. Donegal, rivals Croagh Patrick as a place of pilgrimage. The purgatory itself is a cave, now sealed. Facing page: the lighthouse on Fanad Head, Co. Donegal. Overleaf: (left) Gortin Glen Forest Park, Co. Tyrone, and (right) the sheer cliffs of Achill Island, Co. Mayo.

evious pages: (left) the Georgian mansion of Headfort demesne at Kells, Co. Kerry, the ancestral home of the
arquesses of Headfort, and (right) Achill Head, Co. Mayo. Facing page: low, rocky Slyne Head, off the coast of Co.
alway. Above: the curved stone walls of Dun Aenghus, a massive prehistoric fortress on Inishmore, one of the Aran
ands, Co. Galway. Overleaf: (left) summer sky reflected in the still water of Killarey Harbour, near Leenane, and
ght) a stormy evening sky over Slyne Head, both in Co. Galway.

Facing page: turning hay in Co. Mayo. Above: Doon Point on the Dingle Peninsula, Co. Kerry. Overleaf: (left) the intricate pattern of the stone walls which run across Inisheer, the easternmost of the Aran Islands, and (right) the extensive ruins of the monastery at Clonmacnoise, Co. Offaly, which dates back to the 6th century and steadily increased prestige and importance until the Reformation.

357

Above: the magnificent mansion of Charleville, Co. Offaly, which is considerably younger than its mediaeval appearance would suggest. Facing page: Carton House in Co. Kildare, which was designed by Richard Cassels in 1739. Overleaf: Dublin; (left) O'Connell Bridge crosses the Liffey into broad O'Connell Street and (right) the quadrangles of Trinity College.

Dublin. Above: the Liffey at sunset. Facing page: O'Connell Bridge and the Liffey. Overleaf: some of the many shopfronts and elegant Georgian doors which make Dublin such a colourful and interesting city.

367

Previous pages: Dublin; (left) Trinty College, founded in 1591, and (right) the domed Custom House of 1791 and the
Liffey. Above: Johnstown Castle, which had to be almost entirely rebuilt after Cromwell destroyed it in 1649. Facing
page: the 18th-century mansion at the 34,000 acre Powerscourt demesne, which was designed by Cassels and badly damaged
by fire in 1974. Overleaf: (left) Cork City Harbour and (right) the Cathedral at Cobh, both in Co. Cork.

Previous pages: (left) the President of Ireland's Residence set in the green landscape of Phoenix Park, and (right)
Curraghmore House, seat of the Beresford family, in Co. Waterford. Facing page: the 700-foot-high Cliffs of Moher, Co.
Clare. Above: Fastnet Rock off Co. Cork. Overleaf: (left) the holy mountain of Croagh Patrick and (right) Ashford
Castle, once owned by the Guiness Family and now a hotel, both in Co. Mayo.

Above: the ancient stone circle at Drombeg, Co. Cork. Facing page: Adrigole Harbour on Bantry Bay, Co. Cork. Overleaf: (left) a scene near the Connor Pass and (right) a gushing stream on the Iveragh Peninsula, both in Co. Kerry. Following page: the Cliffs of Moher, Co. Clare.